GETTING HUNGARY

The quest for a simpler life

Jennifer Self

ISBN-13: 9798610193076
ISBN-10:

Cover design by: Art Painter
Library of Congress Control Number: 2018675309
Printed in the United States of America

CONTENTS

For Mum, Nan and Granddad,
You sowed the seeds.

PREFACE

Winter 2014/15

False starts and not-so-extravagant purchases

"Joe, I don't think I can do it".

My heart was slowly sinking with bitter disappointment. I looked out of the train window to an expanse of dreary, sepia blandness. It was late November and we were off to explore a more rural side of Hungary after spending a few enjoyable days in freezing but stunning Budapest. Hungary had been whittled down as the only realistic option for our attempt at a new more self-sufficient life. And even the crumbliest French and Spanish farmhouses were out of our budget, though they were the most romantic and familiar choice. We didn't have much to work with and knew that there was no point having a pile of rubble in a beautiful location in Auvergne or Andalucia with nothing left over to make it look cottage shaped. Or to feed ourselves for that matter. But as much as I wanted to embark on this exciting new project, I couldn't imagine being isolated in the frost-bitten fields of this apparently vast empty land. We called the whole thing off. I reluctantly returned to the security of my nine to five in London and Joe continued his never-ending post-degree job hunt.

It didn't take long for the boredom, restlessness and frustration to set in once again. We'd get impatient in traffic, irritable in crowds and apathetic about going out. We'd watch the news, roll our eyes at whatever ridiculous story was taking centre stage, and joke that we were turning into whinging misanthropists, but actually, it wasn't far from the truth. We'd find ourselves cursing the pressures of modern society and the over-emphasis on money. Get a good job. Buy stuff. Secure a pension. Get a mortgage. Insure everything. Pay your bills. Buy more stuff because that last stuff is now out of date and/or broken. And be happy and brilliant while you're at it - post some smiling snapshots so everyone knows. We were getting swept along with this Sisyphean life, weeks and months passing like minutes, the routine and repetition involved in life seemed to be killing time dead and speeding us towards life's inevitable outcome. Where did the last 10 years go? Why don't we question things more? Why do so many people settle for this pre-determined life of least resistance? Prepackaged. Predictable.

I was in my late thirties, Joe his late twenties. We'd both travelled a fair amount, before and after we met in Lima, Peru, and we both had life experiences that led us to believe we shouldn't focus on a future that might never come. My mum had died in a bike accident on a family holiday a few months before she turned 50 and Joe spent several weeks in a coma as a child, his body totally battered when a drunk driver wiped out their car just before they turned onto their drive. Just a moment and everything is changed. It's such a cliche isn't it, but time is so precious. Time to think. Time to live. Time you can't get back.

Please don't misunderstand me, we're by no means miserable or humourless people and always make the most of any situation we find ourselves in. But we knew it was our own responsibility to step back, simplify and create the kind of life we wouldn't regret living.

It was shortly after Christmas that we received a glossy flyer in the post, forwarded from Joe's mum with a scribbled note saying 'A friend picked this up from a travel fair recently ... thought you might be interested'. It was an advert for a company promoting house sales in Hungary. They arranged viewing holidays with no obligation to buy, put you up in a nice bed and breakfast with views of Lake Balaton and drove you to properties you might be interested in. It seemed like fate, so we booked our second trip to Hungary.

On Valentine's day, we bought a house. It was the second one that we had viewed out of about ten, over two days, but as soon as I had seen the A4 colour printout at the office I had already fallen a little bit in love with it. It was out of our budget and took our savings right down to nothing. It was £12,000. We got home, told our family, I applied for a year sabbatical from work, and we put our UK house on the market. We had everything crossed for a flukey synchronization that would allow us to be gone by the start of the summer.

Despite the fearful questions immediately thrown at us about finances, healthcare, pensions and the language barrier, reactions were surprisingly positive and encouraging. But as things like "that's amazing, good on you, I wish I could do something like that" were said, facial expressions did suggest a little "Are you completely nuts?". It was only my brother, by his own admission having the worst poker face in the world, who screwed up his face in faux pain at the casual risk-taking. "Aaaaargh, I just don't understand how it's going to work!"

And neither did we. But we were looking forward to finding out ...

CHAPTER ONE

July 2015

Getting Hungary

The newly acquired bunch of keys jangled impatiently as Joe attacked the gate lock. This was really happening. Our new home. In Hungary. This was the moment that our adventure became very real - more so than when I handed in my notice to my world-weary and bemused manager, more than when we sold our overpriced little house in suburbia and more, even, than when we emerged from the Eurotunnel for our road trip across Europe to a country we knew very little about. The last few days had been hot and cramped, moving between overstuffed car and over-heated tent during a heatwave sweeping through central Europe. And we'd just been warned about the state of the place by Eniko, the estate agent's translator, but we were committed. We had nowhere else to go, nowhere else to be.

With knotted stomachs, wide grins and then some difficulty using impatient fumbling fingers, the rust-encrusted lock eventually gave way. We swung open the high, spiked metal gate and stepped into the new life that we had left everything else behind for. After apparently being neglected several months prior and left completely to the elements it may not have been everybody's idea of paradise, but the chaotic beauty of it had us smitten at once. Penfold, our two-year-old lurcher, clearly ecstatic to be released from his lead for the first time in two weeks promptly disappeared into a tangle of undergrowth, chasing flies, and resurfaced much later smelling of dill, corn cobs and sunshine. The front of the garden was perhaps once trying to be a lawn, but the earth was dusty and what grass had survived was like straw. A few more steps in and there were tall weeds, herbs and rogue vegetables that had obviously self-seeded from the previous year - dandelions, daisies, grasses, fat hen and hemp plants like huge Christmas trees, dread-locked tomato plants and sprawling strawberry foliage, brambles, pastel flowering bindweed coiled and climbing over tufts of wheat. Any clear view of the house and garden was obscured by our very own jungle, which became taller and more dense the further into the garden we pushed. The concrete paths to the front door and between the main house and ramshackle outhouses provided the only possible clearings by which to explore. Triffid-like grapevines swamped the route to the front of the house and tried their best to strangle the apple, pear and cherry trees. The trees around the garden were loaded with fruit, the cherries were dark and glossy, ripe and delicious, but already being devoured by wasps. There were apples, pears, plums, both sweet and sour cherries, a peach and an apricot tree. A huge walnut tree in next door's garden provided the only scrap of proper shade. We had deliberately settled for a home with a manageable amount of land, but even with our relatively small plot, the boundaries couldn't be seen because of the thick brush and foliage, accentuated by the overgrown neighbouring gardens on almost every side. It was all very different from the drab, brown, bare land we had seen just five months before when we bought the place - but at least we knew what we were dealing with and estimated that we had the equivalent of just under half an acre to work with. Back then we could see it's potential and what we saw on that first day in July had not let us down. Part of us wanted to keep the garden's magical, overgrown magnificence but I'm not sure if that was simply down to the huge amount of work that was about to hit us.

As tends to be standard with Hungarian village properties, there were several wooden outhouses that would once have housed pigs and chickens, the dry corn husks scattered as me-

mentoes. We recalled from our February visit that this particular row of sheds was leaning precariously with an undulating tile roof joining them all together, and always thought that they'd be the first thing to take down for safety's sake; but on giving them a good shove I'm not sure how we could have demolished them ... they didn't budge! We also had a small summer kitchen opposite the main house and an outdoor loo discreetly tucked behind the sheds, which later proved to be less indestructible. The glass had been shattered in the summer kitchen, and the loo, despite its brick exterior, consisted of thoroughly rotten wooden toilet seat, floor and supports. If we had taken the opportunity for a cheeky photo, I would have ended up 30 foot below, peering up from the bottom of the poo-pit. This area of the land was less than appealing, littered with broken concrete, piles of bricks, scraps of metal, plastic, glass and other rubbish. The sheds themselves took shabby-chic to a new level, assembled in a crooked mish-mash of old planks, window frames and door panels. Nails poked out from almost every surface which added to the exciting obstacle course of low door frames and uneven floors.

The house itself looked like a quaint cottage framed as it was by vines and fruit trees, a shallow porch ran around it's 'L' shaped front and it was topped with misaligned terracotta tiles.

The thick mud brick walls seemed sound at the front of the house with none of the concerning cracks that you see in many rural Hungarian houses and the double glazed windows were old-school - two sets of window panes with a generous gap between them. But the glass wasn't broken and the window frames were solid. The outer walls were coated with dusty pink spray paint in some areas, flaky yellow in others with a dark green undercoat. The previous owner, Laszlo, either had difficulty choosing the colour scheme or had run out of pink. He'd also left us some of his very own artwork nailed to the wall by the front door, a crudely traced bo-peep style girl, messily coloured in various shades of dirty brown. It made me feel uneasy so I ripped it down. Due to the price of the house and in keeping with a 'seat of our pants' approach to things we didn't get, and wouldn't get, a survey of the house, so what had became known as 'the big back wall crack' was something that had played on our minds since we viewed and bought the house in February. We had managed to worry it into a size of epic proportions that would need metal pins and huge timber bolsters to fix. However, when we skirted around the concrete ledges of the house to the back wall we were quite pleasantly surprised to see that Laszlo had made only a mildly bodged effort at fixing it, or at least it was nowhere as bad as we had remembered. The house would not be falling down any time soon.

The keys jangled again as we tried to get the right one for the old wooden double-doors among the unnecessarily numerous options available. Stepping into the house from the oppressive summer sun, the cool hit us, as did the powdery turquoise walls. This was Laszlo's kitchen when we visited in winter, but now it was empty of everything but dust and cobwebs. This was the case with the large orange-walled bedroom to the right, the large yellow-walled kitchen to the left and the dark, mustard-brown coloured bathroom that was found through the kitchen. House layout is very different in Hungary to almost every other country I've been to and it would have been difficult to judge what room should be used for what, with the exception of the obvious bathroom, containing a filthy sink, a filthy shower cubicle and yes, a filthy toilet; all illuminated poorly by a tiny window that was obscured by the shower cubicle wall. The kitchen was declared to be so because it had a sink with a cold tap. Nothing else. No draining board. No cupboards or shelves and the floor was a black, smooth surface that looked ready for tiles that hadn't quite made it. There was a hole high in one wall where a flue could be attached through to one of our two chimneys. The middle room would be our lounge, and the orange room our bedroom, due to its size and the fact that it housed a huge ceramic stove heater for use in the harsh winters. And having visited Hungary in both November and February, we knew that the winters could be as cruelly cold as the summer was now blisteringly hot. The only thing in the bedroom other than the dust and crumbling tile skirting boards was a huge poster of an alpine scene glued onto the wall, covering almost half of it. It was a blurred, faded photo and if you looked closely you could find cut-out pictures of sheep, kittens and naked ladies in a creative collage at the foot of the mountains. Needless to say, like Laszlo's other artwork it made us feel a little uneasy, so it was quickly ripped down like a giant band-aid, leaving a big unpainted rectangle of the picture's memory on the huge wall. There was another room accessible only from outside the house, next to the front door, which was also the access to the huge roof space. This room was quickly decided to be our pantry due to its compact size, but also because it was even cooler than the main house. All rooms without exception were coated in the type of sticky grime and grease spots that can't be removed with the quick wipe of a damp cloth and the spiders had decorated every corner, beam, nook and crevice with wispy, dusty webs that gravitated toward you if you got too close. With the house and garden suitably explored, we got the tent out of the car ... and put it up in the bedroom.

We established quickly that we had no running water and that the electricity wasn't connected - the big reel of wire hanging from the post on the driveway was a testament to that. The lack of power didn't faze us - we'd already been camping on our leisurely journey through to Hungary so were equipped with essentials like radio and torches, had a mini solar panel and battery for charging phones, camera and tablet. We were expecting a fairly barren existence until the arrival of the truck containing the worldly belongings from our past life, which turned out to be just a week later. And being mid-summer we had plenty of daylight hours. Water, however, was another matter - at the very least we needed to eat and drink. And preferably use the loo.

The first solution to our water shortage was to go straight to our local shop and buy a multi-pack of bottled water. This we did, and even managed to completely by chance choose the non-fizzy variety, although it would have given a new twist to teeth-brushing had we got it wrong. Our Hungarian stretched to merely 'hello' and 'thank you' at this point, so it was no mean feat jumping this first hurdle. But it was on our return from the shop that we spotted something that looked very much like a water pump in the village square, and further on, nestled behind blooming flower beds, a tap over a pretty little brick fountain ... on testing, they both had running water. Even happier with this result than our non-fizzy bottled water, we walked the few hundred metres back with our empty plastic jerry can, filled it, wandered home and settled in for the evening, confident in the knowledge that we wouldn't dehydrate.

The following day we did another water run, much to the villagers' apparent amusement, and stumbled across a metal manhole cover on the driveway that we couldn't quite believe that we had missed on the previous few outings. Without too much of a protest, I was sent down it to see if this was the magical mains tap for our home's water. It was. We were saved! This would make life a lot more comfortable over the coming days, if not entirely 'normal'. Without electricity it was too dark to use the indoor shower, but the watering cans that we had bought along with other urgent items for those first few weeks from a huge 'Homebase' style store called OBI, became invaluable. Watering can showers were freezing to the point that spontaneous cursing was unavoidable, but so refreshing in the heat that they have restored our fried brains on more than one occasion. God only knows what the neighbours would have made of two crazy English people prancing around swearing in their pants if they had seen us, but we like to think that the cover of the feral grapevines preserved our dignity. Nothing has been mentioned about it to date. Having water also meant that we were able to wash some clothes for the first time in a few weeks. This was done by trampling them in buckets of sudsy water, followed by a clean water rinse or two. This was soon to be known as 'foot laundry' and would remain the preferred technique through the sunshine months given that we had no intention of buying a washing machine. They are big and bulky, cost money to buy and to run, break down and use far more water than necessary. No, foot laundry was the way forward, even it was a little backward.

Strangely enough, it was water that was the link to our first official meeting with our neighbours. As we were fumbling with our broken gate lock one morning after returning from a cool-of-the-morning dog walk, a short, stooped, slightly weather-beaten man had wandered up to the fence between our driveway and his garden and rested his arms on the railings. He was wearing tatty shorts and was bare-chested, his skin was dark from the sun and he had a cigarette hanging from his bottom lip. Some ash had fallen and nestled in his grey chest hair. He had a friendly face, I thought, until his gruff voice shouted: "veez, okay?". Joe and I looked at each other slightly startled, uncertain whether he was angry or just enthusiastic. "Veez, veeeez?" he barked. We made apologetic noises, explaining, in useless English of course, that we didn't understand Hungarian yet and didn't know what he was saying. We shrugged a lot and spoke to each other in English to emphasise our lack of understanding. "Veez, veez?" More shrugging. "Veez nem okay?". We were at a stalemate, so I decided that I'd run into the house and fetch our Hungarian/English dictionary seeing as this particular word was causing all of us so much distress. Just as I returned to a slightly panic-stricken Joe and had finally found the word in the dictionary, a plump, smiling woman in colourful clothes was coming out to join the man in the garden, holding aloft a glass of water. She pointed at it with her other hand, the man said "veeeeez" and as the penny dropped the four of us all chuckled at how stupid the English couple was. They were simply checking that we had managed to turn on our water, after probably seeing us taking our jerry can for walks in the village. We assured them that we were fine and tried our best to introduce ourselves in the clumsiest way possible. And so began the wonderful relationship with our neighbours, Tamas and Margit.

That whole first week was challenging, but the newness of it all and our fresh faced naivete buoyed us through until we hit some semblance of a routine. From the second day, after we'd bought the necessary cleaning equipment the house was wiped, scrubbed, swept, mopped and left to dry time after time until we felt that it would no longer be sticky to the touch. We're not the most neurotic of people when it comes to cleanliness, but we quite strongly believed that 'squalor' was not the vibe that we wanted for our new home. The Hungarian summer was proving to be intensely hot, with the thermo-metre hitting at least 40 most days, so cleaning inside was done during the middle of the day and without exception ended with a watering can shower. We slept in the tent in our bed-room for the sake of both coolness and cleanli-ness, with both the front door and the bedroom door locked. Well, we wanted to make use of our many keys, but in all honesty, we were a little scared of the garden. We hadn't reached the bor-ders of our property yet and our imaginations could only hint at what was lurking in the eight-foot-high vegetation. We cooked in the kitchen using our limited camp kit and used the bath-room only for the toilet.

In the cool of the morning and late in the even-ings we set to the epic task of clearing the weeds from the garden. This was an absolute joy, partly because the main reason for our move was to live a more outdoor life, but also due to the fact that the garden was a treasure trove. We found small self-seeded peach trees that were hid-den beneath the towering fat hen plants, there were a few onions, a small crop of potatoes and a hardy patch of horseradish. The strawberry plot turned out to be massive and very healthy looking, although the fruit had already finished. Some things were a little more sinister though, which added to our initial unease in the garden, before we had got to know, love and well, trust it. Laszlo, the previous owner, had obviously had a very large clear out before he vacated the premises if the size of the scorch marks were anything to go by. As the weeds were cleared and the extent of his fire became clear, we saw that he'd managed to seriously damage an apple tree, two peach trees and killed another peach tree outright. The fire must have stretched to a circle of about ten feet and amongst the ash was smashed glass, wire, bucket handles, numerous nails, cans, bones, teeth and remnants of pill packets, sweet wrappers and cotton buds. We concluded that Laszlo was likely to have been an alcoholic, pyromaniac, hypochondriac with very clean earholes, and hoped desperately that Penfold wouldn't come bounding out of the undergrowth one evening with a human jawbone between his teeth.

Our lack of electricity continued through July and with very little idea when we'd be reconnected, we were forced to get creative. Hot water for washing up was sourced from our black solar shower bag laid out on the concrete in the heat of the day and we used candles in the evening to light our games of scrabble and glasses of cheap but tasty Hungarian wine. Because we couldn't get the internet without electricity and didn't own smartphones we tried several solutions to access our emails and skype-call our family. Initially we went to the mayoral office which had a big '@' sign outside and had a curious encounter which ended with me sitting at the desk of the mayor's secretary sending an email, with her half drunk cup of coffee still steaming on one side of the screen and a picture of her school-uniformed son in a frame on the other. Although they were very friendly and helpful, this wasn't a comfortable scenario and certainly not a long term option, so we began visiting the mayors office after hours and logging into their internet sat on the bench outside the back door. This suited us for a couple of weeks until we were unceremoniously chased away by an employee who seemed to be trying to impress his girlfriend with his newfound authority. Our explanations fell on deaf, unsympathetic, non-English speaking ears, so we left, red-faced and flustered, to search for other options. This came fairly quickly, in the shape of the village library, located on a hidden side street around the corner from our house. Small, single roomed, with a limited collection of faded, communist-era books, they happily provided us with computers and internet for the equivalent of 20 pence per hour. We were connected with the world again! The promised help with the electricity from the Hungarian housing company was not forthcoming, but with few other options we accepted their excuses and reassurances that it would 'not be long now', and 'just another week'. Not wanting to upset them in case they stopped 'helping' us, we took our vengeful pleasures where we could get them. After one of our regular visits to see them for an update and to recharge our gadgets, we accidentally span the car wheels as we reversed, coating the front of their office with a thick spray of muddy water from a recent torrential summer storm. We apologised profusely but sniggered childishly most of the way home.

So now with water, a cleaner albeit scruffy home, means of fulfilling our electrical needs and the recent arrival of a small truck with our furniture, we started to get a little more settled. The tent was packed away and we were grateful to be sleeping in our own bed and able to sit down on chairs again, rather than on the floor or camp stools. Early mornings continued to be spent pulling up giant weeds from their roots. Days were spent in the cooler internal cave that was the house, filling cracks and whitewashing walls whilst dressed only in our underwear due to the heat - the bathroom was the first room to be tackled with any gusto and even after just one coat it looked bigger, cleaner and the spindly-legged spiders were finally taking their cue to vacate. They were reduced to just a few final obstinate families, happily with minimal deaths or forced relocations. Unfortunately, the white paint highlighted our amateur plastering job, but we congratulated ourselves on maintaining a charming rustic style, in keeping with our rural cottage. Late afternoons saw us burning garden scrap and using the embers for dinners cooked over the small fire pit we'd created over the top of Laszlo's scorch marks. This is when the cheap wine resurfaced that saw us into evenings spent watching the stars and playing scrabble and cards by candlelight. It was really a blissful existence. The hugeness of the task ahead somehow took all of the pressure off.

Despite the heat, we still took Penfold for short local walks each day, both for his exercise and for us to familiarise ourselves with the village and villagers. It was returning from one of these walks, on our driveway in fact, when we had the pleasure of meeting a lovely man introducing himself as Andras. Using some English, some Hungarian and lots of wild arm actions (he amusingly always mimed his wife by holding up two large invisible melons, instead of just pointing at his ring finger) he explained that he lived just up the street from us, had a few children our age and that he was a clerk of some sort at the Protestant church. He welcomed us warmly and left us with a large bucket of the most beautiful apricots which seemed to glow luminous orange and tasted of sweet, juicy perfection.

As though not wanting to be outdone, a grinning Tamas later that morning called us over to the gate and loaded us with armfuls of huge luscious tomatoes, frilly lettuce and a giant marrow all from his own garden. This was good. Especially as we had arrived too late in the year to plant anything substantial ourselves. Joe and I had daydreams of moving next to a sweet couple who would not just be accepting of their strange foreign neighbours, but be friendly and look out for us. We thought it might be a little optimistic, but it seemed to be happening. I pinched Joe on the arm for good measure. "Ow, what the hell?" he protested. "Sorry, just checking" I smiled.

Tamas and Margit often caught us coming and going from the gate, as our house was set back from the road and their garden sidled along our driveway. We chuckled that Tamas had taken to combining our names, calling both of us "John", but we quite liked it. Sometimes there's a smile and wave, sometimes a slightly awkward but laughter filled chat and most of the time we ended up juggling some sort of produce as we unlocked the gate to head back inside. It was on one of these occasions that we thought we'd try to ask where we could get some chickens to kick start our humble little homestead - after all, the sheds seemed sturdy enough and chooks wouldn't take much looking after. It would mark a first little step to self-sufficiency. Following some very poor Hungarian and Joe clucking around with his arms and knees bent, Tamas disappeared and came back with a box of eggs from his own hens for us. Hmmmm. We tried again, making sure that we used the word for chicken rather than pumpkin (they're very similar to the uninitiated!) and were led to believe that we could buy 10 very easily, but not the three or so that we wanted to get us started. Tamas held three fingers up at us quizzically and laughed to himself before shaking his head as if wanting just a couple of chickens were the strangest thing he'd heard all year. Our introduction to Hungarian red-tape perhaps, we thought best to leave it for the time being. As if in consolation, Margit came out of the house with a large plastic basin of squat cucumbers, decorated with bulbs of garlic and dill. She gave some instruction, which we were able to follow quite easily having learned some basic words from our grocery receipts, and sent us off to make our very first batch of Hungarian fermented dill pickles. "Prima uborka!" said Tamas, smacking his lips, "First-rate cucumbers!".

We saw quite a lot of Andras that month, because each time we returned his empty bucket, he would visit later that evening, or the next day

with new goodies. We had huge delicious wal
nuts one day, then tomatoes, followed by peppers. He started hanging the bucket on the gate
post if we weren't there - a bottle of homemade
wine. We took to hooking the empty bucket on
the gate to return it, never expecting it to magically refill - but it did - a bottle of homemade
palinka (strong Hungarian spirit). We started
feeling a little weird. Potatoes. Plums. We didn't
want him to feel that he had to keep providing us with goodies, but we also wondered, with
typical Western suspicion, what he might have
wanted in return. We thought we might try and
find him at mass one Sunday, to say thank you
and try to slow the ongoing gifts. But neither I
nor Joe are particularly religious and considered
that maybe we would end up getting ourselves
into more of an uncomfortable situation than
we were currently in. So we wrote a note of
thanks, saying that he had made us feel very
welcome, but that we didn't need any more produce, and left it in the bucket on the gate. No
more refills. No more Andras. We felt horrific. Especially when we were later told that it's really
quite normal for Hungarian villagers to look
after newcomers in this way. We cursed our stupid first-world neurosis, vowed to change and
whenever we saw Andras in later months, over-
compensated with clear, smiley 'hellos' and engaged him in inane conversation as much as possible.

By the end of July we had about a third of the garden cleared of the larger weeds and had laid large tarpaulins on a couple of plots for soil solarisation, in an attempt to kill off the ubiquitous bindweed. We had fixed a leaking mains tap with Tamas's help, and been very impressed at the plumber's £2 fee for labour. Joe had removed the worst of the burnt and decayed limbs from our various fruit trees and we had dug a small, cooling dog pool for Penfold, inspired by the 'hundedouche' we saw in German campsites. We should have predicted that it would be the two us us that ended up using it instead of the dog. Headway was made in the house slowly - mainly with the painting of bathroom and lounge. And I turned my hand to some craft in the evenings, creating a fly-screen for the front door made from empty walnut shells, courtesy of Andras, glued onto lengths of string. It looked beautiful and the sounds of the hollow walnuts bouncing together were really very nice, but it scored zero points for efficacy. I was sure you could hear the high pitched buzzy giggling of the numerous flies as they maneuvered effortlessly between the shells and into the kitchen.

More importantly, as the month progressed we began to feel more relaxed, more familiar with the village and more like this was now home. The first few weeks we felt rather alien, almost apologetic at moving to a place where we were more or less oblivious of the culture, couldn't speak the language and were generally quite paranoid about what we were doing and how we'd be received. We never felt sorry for ourselves though and certainly never had any regrets - we simply tried to get a good balance of keeping our heads down, whilst being friendly to everyone we met. And the more we learned about the village, the country and its people, the more we loved the place. It seemed that our gamble at moving to Hungary almost at random, was paying off already.

Margit's Fermented Uborka

These are the simple instructions that Margit gave me for making the pickled cucumbers that you see sitting outside on every Hungarian windowsill, sideboard and porch in July. There's no vinegar involved, no cooking and no real need to refrigerate so long as you have somewhere cool to store them once fermented. They are packed with probiotic goodies, great for your gut. And actually you can replace the cucumbers with more or less any vegetable that you fancy and add any herbs and spices to your own taste.

Ingredients:
cucumbers
large bunch fresh dill

several cloves garlic
grape leaves (if available)
salt water (about 2 tablespoons salt to each litre water)
sliced bread

Place the washed whole cucumbers in a large clean jar, bowl or pan together with the dill, crushed garlic and grape leaves. The leaves help the cucumbers keep their crunch, but they're not essential. Pour the salt water over the cucumbers so that they are completely covered - this is important to keep the 'wrong' bacteria away from the vegetables. Try not to over-fill your container due to risk of leakage later, during the potentially frothy, bubbly fermentation. Lay the slices of bread over the top of the jar/pan, cover loosely with a lid and put in the sun, or a warm place for several days. The reason for the bread is up for debate - I suspect that the yeast in the bread might help start the ferment, and that the bread once swollen with brine, helps to create a good seal over the vegetables.

You'll see if you're using a glass jar that the water will first go cloudy and bubble, then start to clear again, although in my case not completely. Taste test your cucumbers with clean fingers or fork and when you're happy with the flavour (they will get more sour and 'pickly' the longer you leave them) move them to a cool place. This will stop any further fermentation ... if they ferment for too long they will likely go soft and slimy and although they are still edible, I can imagine the texture could be off-putting for some.

CHAPTER TWO

August 2017

Pantrification

The typical Hungarian village can be a curious and unfamiliar place to the visitor, quite different to other favourite stereotypes across much of Europe. You won't see British style twee thatched cottages, there are no whitewashed stone houses with azure blue shutters as in Greece, nor the chalets of Austria or bright tiling of Spain. Many Hungarian villages on first view are are plain, tatty and utilitarian. They feel empty and, lets be honest, poor. But scratch the surface and they change character before your eyes. Our regular dog-walks became reconnaissance missions that have led us to fall in love with the place and made us thankful that we've broken away from town and village high streets with the same shiny, duplicated shop fronts that lack any quirk or character.

Step outside our gate and walk down the short driveway to our quiet road, we're bordered on one side by Tamas and Margit's garden full of tidy rows of garlic, kohl rabi, carrots, cabbages and neatly raked bare soil. On the right is the home of our more private neighbour, a well maintained but simple single-storey, mud-brick house. Look up the road and there are more of the same houses in various states of repair, close to each other but always with large gardens to the side or rear. Hooked on many fences are crates of, not milk bottles, but soda siphons - apparently so beloved as it was a Hungarian who was the founding father of commercial carbon-ated water. And Hungarians are generally a pat-riotic bunch.

A short hop from our driveway is the main street of the village, a long straight artery bordered by deep storm drains. These spend much of their time dry and empty aside from the odd slinking stray cat, but are crucial for the deluges of water that pour like waterfalls from drainpipes and gutters during the summer storms that seem to be at their peak in August. The houses along the road are on the most part scruffy. They can range from the occasional two-storey new-build with fresh paint, to the down right dangerous - houses that have foot wide and foot deep cracks, crum-bling brick, rickety roofs and large, home-made wooden buttresses keeping them from sliding into a pile. And all inhabited, regardless of the state of disrepair. But on the whole the houses are sound, simple and somewhat threadbare.

The gardens generally are seen as working spaces - they're for fruit, vegetables and animals. The animals are mostly unseen from the road - the chickens will be pecking and scratching around a dusty back yard and pigs rarely see the light of day from their small sheds, only the dogs might be wandering the front garden, if they're lucky enough not to be chained. Front gardens are very often for flowers and Hungarian villagers do flowers very well. From early spring through to late autumn there will be masses of blooms in borders, pots, hanging baskets and everywhere in between. They'll spill over gates, under fences and even take over the sloped sides of the storm drains. The gardens of the village square are always colourful and well tended. Whether its intentional or not, the flowers more than make up for the drabness of the houses and actually, in the bountiful months of summer the scruffiness suddenly becomes organic, beautiful and compliments the lush gardens.

Early in the morning, we're rarely the first up and about. There will almost always be a glimpse of the village's deputy mayor partaking in his dawn run. Tanned and glistening, wearing nothing but his ultra tiny speedos barely visible below his giant taut belly, he'll jog past, sneakers in hand, with a wiggle that is worryingly hypnotic. Sometimes he'll stop for a chat with friends and neighbours whilst stretching out his muscular legs, like its the most normal thing in the world to be out chatting in your pants. Walking along the high street will always involve being passed by several villagers cycling to the bakery for their white rolls, or overtaking them if they've given up on a slight hill and have taken to pushing. Old ladies with shapeless dresses and sagging tights gravitate slowly towards whatever stalls are setting up in the little market square. They turn around and bark with empty gums, while we smile apologetically, not sure if they're angry or pleased to see us. There's a fine line between the two where elderly Hungarians are concerned. Everyone says hello, good morning and most people are cheerful as they set about their day. It sometimes feels like being on a low-budget, European version of 'Last of the Summer Wine' as we wave a hello to the village idiot named 'bread', greet the ruddy-cheeked village drunk Francis who looks just like a dirty santa claus and have the village goat breeder 'Milky Laszlo' tip his hat at us. Its not uncommon to see horses trotting along the main street pulling their carts of hay, firewood or produce - the village apparently used once to be known for its equestrianism.

The aroma of fresh bread, the traditional retes and coffee wafting from the air vents of the bakery are just heavenly and despite our strict budget we find ourselves indulging in the fluffiest loaves with the crispiest crust more than we should. Shops in Hungarian villages are quite strange in that you often can't identify them as shops at all. The bakery or 'pekseg' was clear because apart from the glorious smells, there was an a-board with pictures outside and a statue of a chubby, smiling baker mounted above the door. We spotted the post office or 'postas' from the name and bright green bugle logo and the national tobacconist or 'dohanybolt' from a frontage common across the country, but everything else was pot luck and even now we stumble across shops that we never knew existed. Shops here look like houses - if you're lucky and happen to have a Hungarian/English dictionary in your pocket, they'll have some sort of sign to indicate what they sell, like the 'viragbolt' (flower shop), 'gazdabolt' (literally 'farmer shop' but sell all sorts of hardware) and the numerous 'vegyes-bolt' (the tardis-like 'mixed shop' that is basically a mini-market, and can be found on almost every street). The dentist had a picture of a smiling tooth, so we were fine with that one. And the funeral director an ornate cross. But they are all houses that look exactly like their neighbours. No window displays, no advertising and randomly scattered throughout the village rather than all on the main street. There's a clothes shop that we assume is a clothes shop because they hang a few garments out on their open door, but the garage where we had our car serviced had absolutely nothing. This is the beauty of the Hungarian village you need to know the people and the place to be able to get things done. And its great because it keeps you engaged in your own life, rather than finding yourself wandering zombie-like around over marketed products in over familiar chain stores. After two years its not a surprise for Joe to turn to me and say "We really should use our local animal feed shop to get the chickens grain" and I respond with "We have a local animal feed shop?". "Yeah, it's that house there ... just noticed it". It would be equally unsurprising if we ended up in the dining room of said house with the family staring at us as we smile nervously, apologise and slowly back out of the door.

Moving along the street there is the unavoidable chorus of dogs wreaking havoc as they pass the barking baton from garden to garden in a bizarre noisy relay race. The dogs used to irritate and intimidate us, but with the help of Penfold who remains calm, quiet and totally nonchalant, we've become accustomed to them now and know most of them well albeit by names that we've invented ourselves. They mostly seem happy and excited, simply barking from boredom, although there was one pup we dubbed 'Rasta-dog' on account of his skirt of dread-locked fur, who seemed quite different from the rest. If you could make out his eyes through the thick matted hair, there was an evil stare that was really quite unsettling. It was walking past Rastadog's garden that was the only time that Penfold used to bark back, which antagonised the poor thing further. We were always grateful for the secure gate as we passed his garden, although we've seen examples of a barrier not being necessary at all. On one occasion we were startled by a pair of large aggressive alsations, slathering and growling through the railings at us. We were even more startled when we reached the gate to their garden and it was wide open. There was no time for evasive action at this point, as our blood started pumping ... but it was all rather an anti-climax as the dogs continued to snarl and bark behind an invisible fence, not even attempting to step out of their territory as Penfold glanced at them, yawned and continued on his jaunty way. The alsations' neighbour was a huge tan mastiff who couldn't bark, but chose to wheeze enthusiastically as if it were close enough. And then there are the disappearing old dogs, like Bernie the Great Bernard and Frank the singing husky, who were happily lazing in the garden one day and upgraded for a younger model the next. We've never asked what happens to the old models, but all of our doggy experiences have led to us feeling way more sympathy for them than annoyance.

Further up the road you can see the huge nest of the local stork family atop a lamp post reinforced with a large metal frame for this very purpose, complete with two large uncoordinated chicks waiting for the return of their parents. We have just the one pair of storks in the village, but the nests can be seen throughout Hungary. They're empty from late summer to spring, but during the months in between its not uncommon to be in the garden and have the large pterodactyl-like shadow of the huge birds pass over you. Its impressive no matter how many times you see it. On from here we can turn onto a grid of multiple back roads that lead from the high street through the depths of the village, between gardens that consist of huge crops of paprika and through to the outskirts of the village where the houses get shabbier still and the gardens turn into acres and acres of farmers fields, filled with corn and sunflowers. The roads turn to dust tracks the further away from the main street you get and everything is quieter. The distant barking dogs can still be heard, as can the cockerels, who don't seem to care what time of night or day it is. But another faint sound comes into range, one that could be taken as really quite eerie given a cool morning, an early mist and a deserted street. The closer it gets, the louder it becomes ... children singing, tingling bells and a frustratingly catchy nursery rhyme tune. The bizarre sound is nothing more than the call of the gas van, a little yellow truck that crawls the curbs waiting for customers to pop out from their gate and swap an empty gas canister for a full one. We have several different vans who creep around the streets peddling their wares other than the gas van, there's frozen foods, fish, meat and a separate one for ice-cream that does the rounds a few times a day at this time of the year. And they have all seem to have outdone themselves on the weird music front. I simply love this unapologetic quirkiness of our village and it's about this time of year that you might stumble across one of the stranger events held in the little village square - the annual strongman competition. It took us a fair while to figure out what could possibly happening within the large huddle of grinning villagers, but seeing the collection of heavy tyres, shabby metal weights on unstable-looking poles, an old parked bus attached to a heavy rope, a table full of plastic awards and a guy making announcements through a tinny microphone we finally figured it out. Some unlikely competitors stepped forward, far too old, or too feeble, or too fat to be participating - but fortunately the event progressed hernia free. We walked away chuckling to ourselves, thinking it a fabulous two fingers up to health and safety experts who in the UK would have closed down the event within seconds of it being proposed.

On 20th of the month the whole of Hungary celebrates St Stephen's day - the anniversary of the canonization of King Stephen in 1083 - and if you're lucky enough to be wandering around our village you'll see Hungarian flags together with those bearing the village crest fluttering from lamp posts and trees strewn with red, white and green crepe paper streamers. Shops close early and the sports field hosts a fete bustling with families and friends, beer and wine flowing freely and a big vat of delicious goulash available to everyone who knows how to acquire the appropriate paper chit. There are games, competitions and raffles, musicians and dancers perform in traditional dress and sweet little children bop away innocently to English language pop tunes with x-rated lyrics. The night always finishes with music, dancing and a spectacular fireworks display, the cost of which could probably renovate all of the crumbling buildings of the village.

*****

Returning to the relative calm and tranquility of our own garden, with the sun now warming the ground and the sky an impossible expanse of the brightest blue, we took stock of how our own crops were doing before the heat forced us to shelter inside. One of the joys of giving up full time work on this quest of ours for self-sufficiency has no doubt been the opportunity to stop and smell the roses, or more accurately the peaches. We literally have the time to appreciate the ripening of fruit, the growing of leaves and the swelling of roots. Walking barefoot between the plots we can carefully take account of how dry the earth is, how high the weeds are, if there are any pests starting to cause problems and of course how ready the crops are to harvest; then we take the appropriate course of action. August days generally see a shift from weeding and watering, to spending more time picking and processing. We've learned over the past few summers and autumns, that the preserving of our goodies takes a lot more skill, time and effort than the actual growing of it, especially when you don't have a fridge or freezer. Armed with a bucket, a knife and a garden fork we set to collecting our fruit and vegetables. We slice off courgettes before they morph into marrows, gently ease onions and beet out of their beds, dig for carrots and potatoes like treasure, pick dwarf beans, peppers, cucumbers and huge scarlet tomatoes, cut cabbages, pinch out spinach and chard leaves and select the largest of the corn cobs.

Daily checks and harvesting means that our food is as fresh as possible when we're ready to eat it - the garden keeps everything crisp and nutritious. Our root crops could stay in the ground happily through until at least early autumn, but not everything can just be left to its own devices else we would lose a lot to rotting as well as greedy slugs, snails and birds. From time to time there would be a surfeit of something and this August, way more plentiful than the last, saw the glut of gluts. We managed to preserve the contents of our prolific cabbage plot by shredding, salting and packing them tightly into jars as sauerkraut, but a huge number went into a new favourite Hungarian side dish called csalamade. This turns numerous cabbages, carrots, peppers, cucumbers and onions into a delicious sweet pickled salad with the addition of some sugar, vinegar and spices; the added bonus was that it can keep well for months. Courgettes and tomatoes were the main culprits of this years surplus though - buckets of them picked and stored in the cool, dark pantry until we had to accept that we simply couldn't eat our way through them. The tomatoes were mostly cooked into numerous jars and bottles of passata. Sometimes the tomato would just be stewed down, sweetened and bottled; sometimes courgettes added and blended into a thick mixture; sometimes garlic or chilies added for a bit of variation. While the over-sized pan of tomato sauce bubbled and steamed, a production line of jar and bottle sterilisation was under way using oven or boiling water, to ensure that the passata remained passata and didn't become, as the year before, stinky tomato beer. We've had to admit defeat with previous attempts and now resort to mixing a tomato juice preservative sachet into each batch. It was too heartbreaking pouring away bottle after bottle of sour, fizzy tomato sauce when we knew how delicious the original fruit had been and how much time had been taken to preserve it. We've improved year on year, from less than a 50% success rate with our preserving when we started, we now rarely lose a jar. Once bottled, the passata bottles huddle patiently on the kitchen table, cooling down in preparation for labelling and moving into the pantry for long term safe keeping - a process that we've named 'pantrification'.

Excess tomatoes that escape immediate eating in salads or being cooked and bottled are designated to the solar drier. This is by no means an expensive or technical process. It involves slicing the tomatoes and laying them out somewhere clean in strong sunshine for a couple of days. We did create a little box solar drier from a wooden pallet, which had a clear acrylic top and old curtain netting around the sides to keep flies at bay, but we found that just laying the slices out in the sun was fine enough and then we weren't limited by the size of the box, drying several kilos of fruit at the same time. Courgettes and summer squash were also sliced and dried this way, the only difference being the final method of storage. Some of the dried tomato is stored dry in clean jars, while some has herbs, garlic and oil added to the jar in a kind of marinade, both work well and the tomato slices are delicious in baking, on pizzas and in sauces. The courgettes and squash however, magically rehydrate themselves in a matter of hours, so have to be vacuum packed. Our dry beans (kidney/borlotti/butter) are treated in the same way, sunbaking for a few days before being jarred and pantrified. The onions have normally reached their optimum size by August, so they are lifted, brushed free of mud and left to dry on the concrete for a week or so in order for the skins to dry thoroughly for protection. Then comes the enjoyable task of plaiting their dried leaves together and hanging them under the porch for a further few weeks, where they join the strings of garlic that were lifted in June and the pegged bunches of sage, thyme, oregano and rosemary cut from our small but prolific herb patch. It would be times like this, seeing our cute little cottage draped in our garden's harvest that I would be blanketed with a warm contentment that made it just about okay that our broccoli and cauliflower had failed for the second year in a row.

There are apricots by the kilo at the start of the month but they ripen so quickly that the tree is bare within a week. As if playing a bizarre telepathic game of tag, the next tree to ripen is the peach, followed closely by the pear, plum and grapes. Much of the fruit makes healthy breakfasts and snacks, but there is too much to eat and so begins a seemingly never ending process of making chutneys, jams and compotes. The elderberry overhanging our fence makes a fabulous liqueur when mixed with sugar, rum and chili, but most of it makes our staple winter red wine. We end up with litres of it in the pantry in plastic bottles, ready to be upgraded to mulled wine in December and January. There has been more than one occasion when after making compotes, crumbles and topping up the fruit bowl, I seem to have more fruit than when I started. But its hardly a depressing problem to have to deal with. All of the fruit is delicious and only somewhat insect infected - one of the disadvantages of taking a completely organic and natural approach to our garden. My favourite have to be the peaches. Our peach tree, despite its fire damage from a few years ago, is sublime; producing fruit sweet and juicy like you can normally only find in Mediterranean climes - I had forgotten how good they could taste after years of trying out the bland, dry fruit from supermarkets that never seems to ripen in the fruit bowl . Even eating a couple a day straight from the tree, we quickly realised that we had too much to get through, so gave a big bag to Margit next door, happy that we finally had something good to offer them in return for all of their produce. They were never to be outdone though, and we later got called over for a selection of cakes and a bag of the yellow peppers that are so common here in Hungary.

All of these garden goodies are our raison d'etre - fresh, pickled, dried, jammed and jarred. All stored in the most important room of the house - our pantry. Having furnished it with a couple of flimsy metal shelves initially and then, some six months later, some huge, solid wooden shelves constructed from donated pallets, it is rarely empty. This month it is particularly full of fresh produce picked from our garden with the addition of armfuls of marrows and patty pan squash from next door. There's the ever multiplying passata, the last bottles of homemade elderflower fizz and the early bottles of elderberry wine awaiting their first racking, several shelves of different fruit jams and a few jars of chutney. The pickled cucumbers are way over-represented. We're up to six humongous glass jars of them now mainly because Tamas grows far too many and apparently has no-one else to give them to. He'll offer them at any given opportunity and even when we politely but firmly turn them down he'll sneak as many as possible into buckets of other produce that we've accepted. So we have a ridiculous amount of pickles. We generally try never to say no to next door's offers. The more food that we can preserve the better, and it seems to make them so happy. The only thing we've really said an outright no to was their sorrel, because we were stocked up with lots of veg and didn't really know what we would have done with it anyway. Poor Tamas looked quite crestfallen and declared what we imagined was the Hungarian equivalent for "Well what do you expect me to do with it?".

The pantry acts as our general food cupboard too as we don't have any of the fitted shelving units of a modern kitchen, so things like flour, sugar, rice, canned goods are in there too - we still have to go shopping for basic staples, even at the most fruitful times of the year. The pantry is also a place to store cleaning equipment, pans and gadgets that we don't have room for and a plethora of empty jars and bottles. This is because, in our very first August here, Tamas and Margit asked if we had enough jars, and having accepted the offer of all their remaining fruit when they cleared the tomato patch, we knew we didn't. We've learned to be frugal with our cash and where we can get something for free, we'll generally snap up the offer. This particular snapping up led to a short trip up the road in Tamas's tinny old Suzuki Swift that smokes just a little less than he does. We went to his mother's house which was empty and for sale as she'd passed away, and although the language barrier prevented me from asking any of the questions I'd like to have asked, I assumed that it wasn't that long ago as her little sandals stood neatly just inside the front door. Tamas found the key for the pantry and we loaded up bags full of old dusty jars, bottles and some jars of preserved cherries, the age of which I could only guess at. He talked at me purposefully the whole time, probably suspecting that I didn't really understand, while I replied 'yes' and 'okay' to everything, knowing full well that I didn't understand. It was an interesting experience and that enabled us to continue cooking up creations to see us into the autumn and winter months.

*****

With the pantry being of such importance, we must seem slightly deluded not owning a fridge or freezer, so let me provide a quick explanation. We decided well before selling our house in the UK that we would be moving predominantly for a simpler existence, which included shrugging off many of the trappings of modern day life. After all, many of these gadgets were essentially introduced to free us up so that we could have more time to ... well ... work to pay for them; and although we wouldn't have money coming in, we certainly would have plenty of time. We also didn't want the cost or inconvenience of shipping large electrical appliances across Europe, having to change plugs, add sockets and check outputs, so we left it all - television, washing machine, microwave, fridge freezer (and a lovely big red Smeg one at that!). The fridge was one of the hardest things to contemplate doing without, but when we considered what we'd put in it, we realised we'd be fine. Fruit, veg and eggs are best not refrigerated anyway; jams, chutneys and sauces are fine if kept cool and not contaminated with the dreaded double-dipping (where a dirty knife or spoon is used). The milk we bought in Hungary was UHT, so was fine until opened. We were happy without ice and the water from the tap ran cool enough even in the heat of summer. But we did hit a stumbling block with butter, cheese and on the few occasions that we bought meat ... so we made a fridge. This consisted of a terracotta pot placed inside a slightly larger terracotta pot with sand filling the gap between the two, then the double pot is placed in a shallow tray of water. After a few hours the water is drawn into the terracotta and through a process of evaporation, the space inside the inner pot cools. We drape a teatowel over the top and place our dairy items inside the pot. This has done us well on all but the hottest of summer days, and of course in winter, it's not needed at all as the entire pantry turns into a giant walk-in fridge.

We've never owned a dishwasher so couldn't miss that, but with our lack of kitchen draining board we took to doing the washing up outside at a second hand double sink that we've set into a wooden frame, while the dishes air dry on the wooden table next to it. Its really quite a pleasure washing dishes with the sun on your face, the birds singing and the chickens pecking around your feet. This arrangement lasts all the way through to early winter, but when the extreme cold arrives there's a hiatus until spring, which is when the kitchen table has to suffice. Without a washing machine or dryer the foot laundry and clothes line is still how we clean and dry our clothes and although its one of the jobs that does take significantly longer without the machine, it's become a normal weekly routine and not at all hated as we thought it might. Given the choice of doing a few loads of foot laundry or being back in my office, staring out at London City Airport, pondering on the point of it all, I'd choose the laundry every time. What has made this task easier though is the arrival of a 1950s mangle. I never saw myself as the kind of person who would be happy to receive a mangle as a 40th birthday present, but I was ecstatic, and the fact that it's an Acme branded one, as if sourced from a Wile E.Coyote cartoon, made it all the better. No more contorted hands from wringing clothes, and they dry much faster to boot. For the sake of full disclosure I will admit that our clothes are not washed to everyone's standard and we're having to phase out our lighter clothing as we always have trouble getting our whites white enough. But the clothes are definitely clean, if not bleached bright, and there's something about the smell of sun drenched, air dried sheets and towels that comforts the soul.

August is a month of mowing. The combination of heavy rain and prolonged periods of sunshine makes our grass grow at a ridiculous rate and even though our lawn is far from bowling green standard (it's getting a little thicker and greener from year to year from the dust-bowl it once was), it still needs attention. In keeping with our avoidance of expensive electrical gadgets, the first mower we bought was manual, with blades inside a barrel, that needed pushing vigorously to work as the ground was so lumpy. It was cheap to buy, cost nothing to run, had no annoying cables and actually did leave the garden looking a lot tidier. But it was hard work, couldn't handle grass that was too long and it was noisy. Embarrassingly so. We couldn't mow the grass on the driveway without Tamas coming out to watch and chuckle, cigarette in hand like it was some sort of peculiar spectator sport. He would stay for a while before offering to do it for us with his big electrical machine, which we at first were grateful for, but then realised that this wasn't our preferred solution. We don't like to take advantage and also wanted our lawn care independence. Over the course of a year the manual mower got more battered and blunt, so we gave in to a strimmer at first and then a cheap electric mower and a couple of 30 metre extension chords. Its done us well so far, but we just don't get the same full body workout.

*****

It was the August of this year that saw us host our first guests from Warm Showers, an online community who provide free accommodation for cyclists. On an altruistic level, it's great to share what we're doing with others, to show how living simply can bring such joy and to spread our little messages of self-sufficiency and care for the environment. However, it was the social side of hosting that was incredibly valuable for us, living as we do with such limited contact with others, especially English speaking others. We're both generally quite sociable people and are both well travelled, so our somewhat static, isolated lifestyle can sometimes take its toll, but this was a chance to meet new people, talk about our passions of cycling and travelling, and pretend that we have a social life for a night. Hosting strangers could take a lot of trust and some people's reactions to the arrangement have them wondering why you would do this for free when there's the possibility to make money. But our experience so far has been nothing but positive and we're happy to continue reducing the use of money in our life. It felt like the most natural thing in the world offering people who are tired and hungry a place to stay and a plate of food, like this is how the world should be all the time, everywhere. A little bit of love for your fellow man.

Our first visitors were a French couple, who arrived late, tired and hungry with a soaking wet tent from the previous night's rain. It felt a little odd welcoming complete strangers into our home, but we soon got chatting, hung their tent out to dry, explaining that they were welcome to use our little spare bedroom made from the summer kitchen building and that we had plenty of food for them when they were ready. There's no obligation to feed your Warm Showers guests, but we had so much to spare it seemed ridiculous not offering it, so after they were refreshed we all sat down for a meal of various salads, freshly baked bread and cherry wine, all proudly homemade. We hoped that we'd gone a little way to make their tour through an obscure section of rural Hungary a little memorable and were pretty sure that they felt comfortable when the guy fell asleep at the table mid-conversation. Our second guest, a young, tattooed Italian guy, stayed with us for a couple of nights which is unusual, but he was here to sell his home-made jewellery at the nearby Ozora festival rather than passing through. Again, it was an enjoyable and relaxed time, sharing our food and space with someone in exchange for their stories and company. He even joined us for a dog-walk around the village before he left, cycling bare-foot and bare-chested back to Italy.

Csalamade (Hungarian Mixed Pickles)

We love sampling local Hungarian village restaurants - etterem, vendeglo or csarda - often family run places with traditional decor, checked tablecloths and verandas full of flowers. The fare is simple, hearty, delicious and often incredibly cheap with the 'napi menu' (the daily set lunch) costing just a few pounds for a bowl of soup and main meal. There will no doubt be plenty of juicy, salty meat on the menu too which pairs up wonderfully with assorted pickles that most Hungarians seem to love.

Variations of this sweet and crunchy mixed pickle can be found on most menus. It seems to be different every time, but always just as delicious. It's easy to make, simple to tweak to your own preferences, uses up bumper crops nicely and can store through to at least mid-winter.

Ingredients:
cabbage
carrot
pepper
cucumber
onion
salt
apple/cider vinegar

sugar
herbs - e.g. dill, bay leaf
spices - e.g. mustard and coriander seeds, peppercorns, chilli, clove, ginger, allspice

Finely slice all of the vegetables, sprinkle with salt (about a tablespoon per large bowl of veg), scrunch together with your hands and leave to one side, covered, for an hour or so. This softens the vegetables and gets them juicy.

In the meantime, mix a tablespoon of sugar per 100ml of vinegar and add the herbs and spices that you would prefer - I throw in a pinch of everything. Taste the mixture and adjust to your own preference, you may want it sweeter, or hotter, it's up to you.

When the vegetables have wilted slightly, add the spice mixture and toss together. Pack tightly into sterilised jars and top up with spiced juice mix from the bowl. The pickle is ready to eat straight away, but as long as its submerged in the pickle mixture it should keep well for many months in a cool place.

CHAPTER THREE

September 2015

Let there be light!

Nights were shortening but the sun remained warm as September rolled into our scruffy little homestead. Still without electricity after eight weeks, we were starting to prickle with frustration at the uncertainty of when we might be connected with the world again. Fortunately, this was when we stumbled across our unlikely Hungarian hero and new friend, Sandor.

It all started when I noticed that the undercarriage of the car seemed to be wanting to detach itself and on closer inspection found the front plastic wheel arch was loose, frayed and resting on the tyre and grass below it. The car had done so well hauling us and our gear across Europe and was still driving beautifully despite the incredible heat she had endured and minor damage that we had unwittingly inflicted, but now it seemed was time to give her a little TLC. Knowing that we had limited funds that wouldn't really stretch to even an 'old' new car, we made a pact with her early on that if she looked after us, we'd return the favour, so without too much deliberation we drove her the short distance to what we hoped was a garage and spare parts workshop at the end of the village. Joe and I were all ready for some charades of epic proportions, but the receptionist took note of the language barrier, paused us politely and called through to the office for someone else to help. Sandor was a tall, well-built, smartly dressed man of about middle-age; lightly tanned, balding and wearing a concerned look, but contagiously warm smile. He seemed ecstatic to be given a chance to practice his English, although the enthusiasm with which he spoke it did nothing to improve its rustiness. He helped us enormously, inspecting the car, ordering the relevant parts, offering to help fit them the next day and assuring us that we had a car jack under the spare wheel when we were convinced that we didn't. He spoke confidently and with many more words than were entirely necessary, veering off onto numerous tangents, just to be sure that his language skills were getting a proper airing. He was fascinated that two English people would come to live in a small rural village and could not grasp why or how we would succeed in our plans to stay, explaining that we must learn Hungarian and get jobs as soon as possible, both of which would be incredibly difficult for us. He continued smiling encouragingly as he told us how we probably wouldn't last the harsh winter, should lock everything up because of potentially violent thieves and muttered various other sweet nothings to cast clouds over our dreams of self-sufficiency.

Late the following afternoon Sandor arrived at our house as promised, with the ordered car parts and some appropriate tools. His post-work look was more dishevelled than we'd seen prior, a look that we came to associate with him more and more as we grew to know him better ... on this occasion, he was smeared liberally with black engine oil with his shirt half untucked, but his smile still in place. He explained that his 'father-in-love' (his wife's father) had a house just around the corner, which had a mechanic's car pit where it would be easier to access the underside of the car. Joe being male, and rural Hungary being stuck firmly in the 1950's equality-wise, he was invited to help out, as Sandor accepted a quick sugary coffee and gave a brief muddled speech about Hungarian history. He repeated the urgent need to learn Hungarian and get jobs and left, Joe following on his heels, to my smirk and raised eyebrows.

Joe returned late that evening. I was at the point of worrying that he had very trustingly wandered to a stranger's house and had images of calling his folks in England trying to explain his disappearance. But at dusk, the gate clanked and he bounced in grinning, covered in the same grease that had coated Sandor earlier. They hadn't finished with the car but were making good progress, and they had bonded over life stories and the discovery of the jack under the spare tyre. Sandor had also taken pity on our electricity shortage and had apparently taken it upon himself to take charge of the situation.

Over the following weeks, Sandor proved invaluable. Slowly, slowly catchy monkey as they say. In this case, very slowly. And one very small monkey at a time. Paperwork from the electric company had arrived in the post, consisting of numerous forms, information and instructions in what seemed to be overly convoluted and officious Hungarian. We had contacted Eniko from the housing agency, but were now very impatient with the constant advice to be patient and so took the opportunity to cross-reference our information. Several phone calls by Sandor later we discovered that the electricity had been disconnected because Laszlo had managed to accrue a massive debt of unpaid bills in his last few months at the house, which we may or may not have to pay in order to be reconnected. There was also the matter of having to install a new switchboard that met safety standards and the reconnection fee itself. The cost was mounting up horrendously ... and all of it unexpected, as we were sold a house that was good to go power-wise. Sandor was fuming on our behalf. He was angry at both the situation and the lack of help from the agency, and couldn't believe how long we'd waited and how calm we were. We remained just a little bewildered - we knew there'd be teething issues at some point during our adventure, just not the shape or size of the teeth.

"Let's see. We will go to the shop and you will be angry with them. We must be fighting" declared an animated Sandor. "You must show them you are not happy. You must be angry like a, let's see, what is this animal with the spines, that is into a ball and sniffing and digs in the ground?"

"A porcupine, oh wait ... not a hedgehog?" attempted Joe, with a combined look of bafflement and amusement, enjoying the game.

"Yes, yes, yes, let's see, you should be angry like a hedgehog!"

The ball was finally rolling and we were told that when we'd signed the appropriate forms and obtained the correct papers and got bits of them stamped at various offices in different towns, that an electrician might possibly call to see us at some point soonish. The debt had been resolved one way or another. Despite Sandor's best efforts we never had serious fallings out with the housing agency, but we did manage to get them to pay for half of the reconnection fee, an amount which we inflated heftily so as to get as much covered as possible. Perhaps we should have fought for a better outcome, but we felt that it wasn't the time to make enemies of our fellow countrymen, and we had more interesting and important things to focus on. Like actually getting the electricity connected.

A week after faffing with money and forms we were still none the wiser about a connection date. It felt closer but there was no certainty, so we thought we'd take matters into our own hands. We had of course considered solar panels, but after some research it became clear that the cost of installation and rewiring an old mud house may not be the best option for us immediately, particularly as we wouldn't need much electricity anyway. We would think about that another time. But after a trip to the OBI hardware store, we did find ourselves unboxing a big shiny new generator on the porch. We thought it was a fabulous idea, regaining control and being able to be off-grid would have really suited us, especially given the current ridiculous circumstances. We were so engrossed in discovering how it might work and finding out that it probably wasn't the right machine for our needs, that we hadn't noticed that Sandor had wandered into the garden and was looming over us looking absolutely horrified - "Let's see. How much was this? You must take it back. Now. You don't need this. You'll have electricity next week. How much was it? Take it back!"

We shrank guiltily from his questions, trying to explain our reasoning, but Sandor wasn't interested. He had dates for us. The electrician would be with us the following week and the electricity company would turn the power on a few days after that. One more week. We conceded defeat and promised that we'd take the generator back ... which we did later that day, fortunately with a full refund. We thanked Sandor profusely as he began a long, convoluted dialogue about how beneficial it would be for me to change my name to something more Hungarian.

It was a total of ten weeks, in mid-September, that the magic of electricity was delivered to the house. The hot water tank in the bathroom clunked, tapped and hissed to life, simultaneous charging of gadgets began and a date was set for the phone line and internet to be installed. On that first evening, I must have spent at least ten minutes flicking the wall switches on and off, grinning maniacally at the miracle of light while repeating 'ta-daaa!' in my head.

Life didn't change too drastically once everything was connected. Having said that, the lights after dark were appreciated more than I had thought. I would never want to repeat the need to clean up after Joe by torchlight as he stationed himself on all fours half-in and half-out of our only exit in a stubborn, albeit rare, drunken stupor. We could now cook our tea later in the evening and the greatest boon was being able to contact friends and family whenever we wanted, without the inconvenience of grabbing stealth internet access wherever possible. Sandor continued to visit us on a daily basis after his working day, to see if he could help us, to practice his English and ask if we'd yet found any jobs. He'd walk his bike up the drive, lean it precariously against our neighbour's fence and give us a shout before letting himself in the gate. Penfold would always greet him excitedly, running in circles and jumping so high that they'd nearly touch noses, only for him to get a whomp to the snout as Sandor clumsily brushed him aside. He'd always go back for more though. Sometimes Sandor would accept a tea or coffee, and he would always accept food, even if he had no idea what he was being offered. There were so many questions that he answered for us and so many really quite huge favours that he gladly involved himself in that we eventually felt concerned that he might get in trouble with his work ... or even worse, his wife. One evening he popped round to help start the process of getting our car re-registered and to try pushing us one last time into having a big argument about the electricity. This was the point at which we realised that he liked coming to see us though, as he had started letting himself in the gate unannounced and on this occasion took a seat on the sofa, picked up Joe's guitar and started playing 'House of the Rising Sun' before saying that he really must go as he should visit his sick 'father-in-love'.

*****

September was when the house finally felt that it was taking on some of the responsibility of being a real home. The bathroom had put up some serious resistance for a long time, for after the minor cracks were filled, the walls given several whitewashes and the ceiling boards gloss-painted, we still had the issue of a huge, ugly, brittle plastic shower cubicle in the centre of the room. We wanted to take it out mainly because of the need to allow some natural light to penetrate the room, but also because it was mould-infested, smelled fusty and we longed for a bathtub. This shower however, was stubborn. It was both screwed and plumbed into the wall, cemented to the floor and wedged firmly against the roofs wooden beams. In total it took us over six weeks of prodding and procrastination to remove it, slowly chipping away between episodes of utter frustration using every wrench, screwdriver, crowbar, hacksaw, lump hammer and any other random tool that came to hand. Eventually, in one particularly determined attempt, the frame of the cubicle came loose, the mains water was turned off and the whole bulk of the shower could be prized away from the wall to be dismantled and dumped unceremoniously behind the sheds. The change to the bathroom was incredible. Even though the window was tiny and deep-set, daylight poured in and illuminated the now light, bright walls and turned the room into a big, fresh space worthy of our ablutions. The base of the shower was the next thing to go, leaving us with an amount of tubing protruding from the drainage hole and a big area for us to place and plumb in a new bath when we got around to buying one and researching some basic plumbing skills. The floor was flat, a mixture of old tiles and concrete patches and although not exactly pretty, it was at least a little rustic and soon to be covered with an assortment of bathmats from one of our removals boxes. The bathroom was finished off with some tiling at the back of the sink; and blue paint around door and window frames and roof beams, all completed while wearing the traditional attire of the painter - bra and knickers. It was still too hot for clothing, plus gloss paint is my nemesis and this new approach prevented me from smearing it around the rest of the house, garden and dog. And so, the first room of the house was mostly done.

The plastering and painting progressed steadily from room to room. After the bathroom came the lounge and pantry. The walls were sturdy for the most part, with scattered cracks of a few millimetres width and only small patches around the base of the walls that needed some real reconstruction. In some cases it looked fine until removing the tiles that had been used for skirting boards, but from time to time, we'd be left with powdery craters that needed building up with increasing layers of plaster over several days. We were proud of our half decent job, costing only the price of a few bags of plaster. And all this done with a little red plastic trug brought from home, two scavenged plasterers' floats from our garden and a dessert spoon which had accidentally made its way home from my work locker several months earlier. A spoon had never been so handy. Forget soups and puddings, this spoon has plastered two rooms, part tiled a bathroom and filled most cracks in our external wall. It deserved mounting, but we still needed it too much.

The rest of the house started coming together too, with the aid of a new discovery. Ozora is a village located about 20 minutes away from us through pretty countryside on small potholed lanes. It's best known for a huge psychedelic music festival that takes over the area for a week every August, which we can hear from our garden given a favourable wind, or unfavourable, depending on your appreciation for electronic music. But Ozora also transforms itself every weekend into a flea market wonderland, where behind every gate awaits piles of spare wheels, lawnmowers, bikes and fabrics. There are toys and clothes, kitchenware and tools, furniture and rugs, all laid out lovingly by the owners of the gardens. Over the course of the month, we acquired four huge beautiful Persian rugs to cover the bedroom floor, a set of heavy woollen curtains to help keep in the warmth in winter, a big mirror for the bathroom and a chunky farmhouse style kitchen table and chairs. All second hand but good quality and all at very good prices, even if we allow for some haggling failures and the obligatory 'unwitting foreigner tax' that can sometimes apply in these circumstances. With a lick of varnish, a few decorative stitches and some cleaning our purchases fit in perfectly. Our house was gradually becoming very homely.

Feelings of paranoia about the stability of the house were beginning to ebb away at this point too, the thick walls gave us no cause for concern, the windows were perfectly fine after a quick sanding and coat of gloss and the guttering proved to be sturdy. The roof, though, was a slightly different matter, particularly given that ours was a layer of seemingly precariously placed tiling on wooden beams. Our house's roof insulation was in the loft floor, a foot or more of packed earth between the big wooden rafters. We had no felt layer or any protection beneath the tiles themselves and on sunny days numerous beams of light broke across the dusty loft space in twinkling shards. Because of this, after any heavy rain we'd taken to inspecting the roof space for drips, which there were, but on such a small scale that a couple of old jars did the job of collecting any leakage. Joe had wanted to venture up onto the roof, but I wasn't so keen on the precariousness of his plan and the possibility of hospital involvement. We told ourselves that we'd just keep an eye on it. Through summer we had a couple of storms of biblical proportions, but it was during one in September that we went into the roof during a storm rather than after it and saw the leakage in its full watery glory. It happened to be at 3am and was by torchlight. Joe had been restless as soon as the thunder had started to rumble in and after a good amount of persuading managed to drag me out of my slumber and accompany him to check things out. As sleepy as we were, we managed to grab a big marker pen and fumbled around the roof drawing arrows pointing to the gaps in the tiles where water was pouring through, whilst repositioning buckets and jars to lessen any water damage. The next day involved purchasing three big cans of expanding foam, all of which Joe used on the marked up areas as if going around icing a giant cake. The stuff looked unsightly and got everywhere, but seemed to do the trick if the next downpour was anything to go by. To be extra sure that the earthen loft floor was protected from any further leaks we used the abundance of plastic coated packing wrap from the removals company, laying it like matting across the entire floor. We'd also spotted a wooden cross beam that was slightly waterlogged and starting to show signs of rot, so that was splinted with some spare wood. Overall it was a solid days work, but worth it as we found that it could be quite draining worrying about minor things like your roof and walls falling on your head from water damage. And we had no hospital visits, although Joe managed to stab himself in the hand with a Stanley knife at some point ... but that was repaired quite easily with a plaster and a cup of sugary tea.

*****

Sandor's regular lunchtime and evening visits continued and he seemed to grow ever more unkempt with every encounter. We took it as a sign of comfortable familiarity that he would turn up filthy, with buttons missing and his shirt more often than not tucked into his underpants, which in turn would be riding above the waistline of his trousers, but in reality, he was probably keeping himself just a bit too busy. Between delivering bitesize chunks of Hungarian history, culture and politics he would nonchalantly slip in a comment about how his wife was a bit stupid and a bit lazy. It became abundantly clear that he was most relaxed when he wasn't actually at home and we were generally happy to keep him entertained. Every now and then he would overstep the mark a little with his assertive advice. Like the time he had come over to let us know that he had, as requested, kindly arranged for a huge wood delivery in preparation for winter, but got distracted by the grass that we had deliberately let grow around grapevines in front of the house, to protect the earth from the sun and rain. He knelt himself down and started tearing heavy-handedly at everything that wasn't a vine, declaring "You must eliminate this, and eliminate this. Eliminate!" like a strange weed detesting Dalek. But his often over-bearing nature was fairly easy to forgive. We knew he didn't entirely understand our approach to most things and given the slightest opportunity would have driven his tractor into our garden and tried to plough the whole area for us, lawn, fruit trees, the lot. Just because that's the way things are usually done here. But his assistance always well outweighed his domineering but well-meant advice.

Our relationship with Tamas and Margit grew stronger, still at this point entirely based on their trying their very best to look after us by force feeding us whatever they could from their excess crops. Early one afternoon, having made a delicious batch of elderberry liqueur from our garden's berries and apples with added chilli, rum and spices, we thought we'd return the love to our neighbours and took them a small bottle of this sticky treat. I'm not sure whether Tamas knew it was homemade or not, but he refused it with such vehemence that we immediately thought we'd done something wrong. Was he angry that he was being gifted something that was essentially from his own garden (the elder-berries, strictly speaking, were overhanging from the very back of his garden) or was it some unspoken but well known Hungarian rule that you never try to gift back to the gifter. We were a little puzzled ... and a little disheartened. While sitting on the kitchen floor later that afternoon, peeling tomatoes ready for a final batch of pas-sata and feeling a bit like we'd let ourselves down, Joe came running in with a large lump of something nondescript but smelling beautifully smoky. In a fluster he shouts that we've been given some smoked cheese, plonked it onto the table and run out again muttering that Tamas has got something else for us too. I took a look and then a poke at the nondescript lump and dis-covered that it was a chunk of smoked, salted pork belly, no doubt from their very own pigs, whose stinky gas wafts into our kitchen at the same time every afternoon. I was filled with a surge of relief - hooray for pork belly and hooray for not offending the neighbours!

We were still making our way steadily through clearing the undergrowth in September and delighting in the plethora of wildlife we were stumbling across as we worked - there were sunbathing lizards, camouflaged preying mantis and stick insects, the most bizarre but beautiful-shelled bugs, all sorts of different birds and butterflies, numerous bees enjoying the assorted blooming wildflowers and a couple of well-hidden wasp nests, one of which Joe accidentally dug up when removing a particularly tenacious tap-root. The wasps retaliated ferociously, a few heading straight up his trouser leg and doing what angry wasps do best. The first I knew about it was Joe running past me at quite a speed, swearing frantically whilst ripping at his clothes. He suffered from multiple stings which gave him swollen legs and made him feel quite unwell for a couple of days, but we avoided hospitalisation once again helped by the tried and tested bed-rest and cups of sugary tea. Fortunately, he was back on his feet again by the time a sizeable truck arrived with our firewood. We weren't too sure what to expect for our equivalent of £500 as all of the weights, measures and sizes really didn't mean too much to us at this point. But what we saw arrive had us staring open-mouthed for quite some time, while Sandor took it upon himself to direct the driver as he backed slowly and precariously through the gate. The truck was very nearly the size of the house and as it reversed, blotted out the sunlight as I cowered in the bedroom, fearful of what carnage those giant wheels might do to the garden and whether the crane attached to it would actually wipe out the little summer kitchen that suddenly found itself in the way of this monster. Joe and Sandor oversaw the unloading, the massive metal neck and teeth of the crane working surprisingly deftly to create several neat mountains of logs, each just over a metre in length and ranging in girth from the size of a leg to the size of, well, a very big tree. After an hour or two we had an area of wood that covered about five square metres of the garden - fortunately an area that we had no intention of using for planting, or anything else, for quite a while. And good job, because little did we know at the time, but that load would last us for four winters and the log-piled area would not really be accessible at all for two. Once the truck had left, leaving deep trenches in the ground where the wheels had been so weighed down, we covered as many woodpiles as we could with tarpaulins to keep it dry, and stacked as many of the smaller logs as possible into one of our empty shed spaces. We wondered how the huge logs would be transformed into wood-burner sized chunks with our complete lack of, and reasonable wariness of any chainsaws - we'd only ever bought pre-chopped wood for fires in the past and didn't even own a decent axe at this point. We looked over to Sandor for guidance, but he was engaged in a deep and rather agitated conversation with Tamas and Margit across our gate. There was a lot of gesturing in our direction and raised voices that did nothing to reassure us that we weren't in some sort of trouble or had offended them in some way. We later found that they had been discussing how furious that they had been at our being without electricity for so long and disgusted that we had paid double what the house was worth - the three of them were clearly angry like hedgehogs. But even with this sudden news, we couldn't be too upset - so we'd paid £12,000 for a £6,000 house. We still had a home and large garden for less than the price of a second-hand car back in England. They all eventually stepped away from the fence, Sandor declared that he would be over in the next few days with his chainsaw to help us and left, wheeling his old creaky bike alongside him.

'Medicinal' Elderberry Liqueur

Sprays of little black elderberries cover the bushy hedgerows throughout the countryside by late summer, but we also have plenty at the bottom of our garden, most of which find their way into the brew we make for our winter mulled wine. But before we get onto winemaking, we use some to make this supposedly immune-system boosting liqueur. I can't guarantee a cure for colds and flu, but as a taken neat it's certainly soothed a few sore throats and cleared some winter sniffles ... and failing that, it tastes pretty good mixed with hot water as a hot toddy which will warm the coldest of cockles on a cold, damp winter's day.

ingredients:
250g apples
400g elderberries
500g sugar
dried chilli
300ml water
100ml rum

Wash and chop the whole apples - there's no need to peel and core as the brew will be strained later - and add to a large pan with everything else except the rum. We recommend roughly two teaspoons of dried chilli flakes, about the equivalent of two chillies. This gives a nice warm glow without burning your mouth off, but you can alter this according to your chilli tolerance. Heat and stir the mixture until boiling, then simmer for just five minutes. Strain the mixture, add the rum and pour into sterilised bottles. This liqueur should keep in a cool place for at least a year ... although we have a batch that has kept well for considerably longer than this!

CHAPTER FOUR

October 2016

The wrong goat and other animals

Goat was our goat. She had long brown hair, a narrow, serious face, was partial to potatoes and had a worrying habit of choking on her hay until it was regurgitated back into her mouth for further chewing. She was the strong silent type, docile enough but wouldn't stand for any nonsense. This is probably why she spent the first few days of our relationship kicking at our hands and fidgeting at our initial attempts at milking, which resulted in only just enough milk to whiten our tea. Cow was also our goat. She was black and white and fairly bovine-looking in her bulk. A stubborn, mischievous but affectionate girl who loved nothing more than standing on her tree stump in the centre of the small paddock that we had created on the sprawling strawberry patch from various scavenged posts and some wire fencing. Now and then she'd close her eyes, stretch her neck and swing her broad face to and fro, which looked particularly comical if the long hairs around her big pink nostrils were dusted with the baking soda that we kept in a dish for them to self administer for digestion. Cow had a black, low slung udder with two huge teats that didn't look unlike Madonna's conical bra strapped to her underside. And from these teats we easily milked a generous litre of milk every morning and every evening.

I had always considered animals integral to a successful, self-sufficient homestead - in my happy, rose-tinted daydreams I tended to a plethora of smiling, fluffy, productive animals pecking, grazing and generally lounging around in their comfy, golden straw strewn pens. But in reality Joe and I had a combined experience of absolutely zero when it came to farmyard animal care - I'd never owned more than one lazy, spoiled cat at a time ... or currently the one lazy, spoiled dog. What we lacked in experience though, we more than made up for in spare time in which we Googled, Youtubed and obsessively flicked through our tattered old John Seymour book on how to become livestock gurus. By our second autumn in Hungary we had accumulated a shed full of chickens for eggs, a shed full of rabbits for meat and some accidental kittens who happened to fall from next door's roof. We almost had the complete set of expected livestock, so it made sense to add a dairy goat into the mix ... and although we ended up with two through our own stupidity, really it worked out for the best as Cow and Goat adored each other.

It was a cool, bright Wednesday afternoon in early October that we had the bizarre experience of goat try-before-you-buy and since then the onslaught of goat-related education had been unrelenting. Our friend Sandor had found someone in the village looking to sell their goats - they were about five years old, currently milking, but also pregnant so we could continue milking for a further year after their kids were born in Spring, and at the equivalent of about £40 each, they were a bargain. Buying local also meant that we could walk our goat home at our own leisure rather than all of us having the trauma of a bumpy road-trip from some far-flung animal market, goat wedged in car boot, bleating at the top of her lungs. We arranged a visit to see the goat, one of three healthy and content looking animals, who seemed more than happy to be milked for us as she chewed loudly on a mix of cereal and seeds. After a quick mooch around the guy's sheds, we asked the owner and his wife numerous questions and at the end of his very speedy milking session, he took the pan into the house and returned with two still-warm glasses of frothy, pure-white milk for us to try. Initially I felt a little queasy about drinking the raw milk, especially because the now flaccid udders from which it had just been drawn were just feet away from me, but it tasted wonderful. Lighter than cow's milk but still creamy and the freshness was obvious. We were sold. In fact, we were so excited after seeing her that, after wiping our milk moustaches onto our sleeves, we decided we would go ahead and buy her instead of waiting to check out what was at the animal market that weekend.

The following afternoon we collected our goat, paid our money and strolled the twenty minutes home. Taking a goat for a walk is probably one of the stranger things we've done since moving into the village, but none of the locals flinched as we trotted past. The goat seemed relaxed and made good speed despite not knowing where she was going, her udder swinging so pendulously that we were forced to slow to grazing speed several times in case of injury. We made it to her paddock in one piece where she set about devouring the readied pile of grass, choking on it a few times and occasionally calling out loudly to assert her presence to a curious Penfold. It was after about half an hour of looking at our new purchase I tentatively suggested to Joe that we had bought the wrong goat. He wasn't convinced, but I could have sworn that 'our' goat should have had a black and white face, big pink nostrils and a gormless grin. Nevertheless, we proceeded with our first attempt at milking in the paddock, which was inelegantly done and amounted to a meagre half cup. I still thought we had the wrong goat, but we made our excuses that she was probably a little stressed from her change of environment and left her to settle, checking on her anxiously every hour like new parents with their first child ... although in our case it was to check she wasn't tangled in her chain or escaping to eat the cherry trees.

It was when we had again milked less than half a cup from our goat the next morning that I managed to convince Joe that things weren't quite right and we put our concerns to Sandor, who called up the seller and explained that we had taken the wrong goat. It seemed like the seller knew fully well that we had taken the wrong goat, but was reluctant to give us the right goat because we were stupid enough to take the wrong goat in the first place. This was probably fair - we should have noticed that one was brown haired with short ears and one was black and white with long ears, amongst other obvious differences, but in our defence we had spent just ten excited minutes with them, mostly staring at their udders and we trusted that the guy would present us with the sampled goat. The problem by now was that the right goat had been promised to someone else so he was not happy to exchange. He offered our money back, but by this time we were quite attached to the wrong goat. And so over the course of a few days, we started discussing the benefits of buying two goats, the right goat and the wrong goat, if the seller was OK with that. Fortunately he was and, after another precariously speedy walk home involving the goat continuously kicking herself in the udder, they were reunited and appeared to be very happy indeed to be together again, after a display of extravagant headbutting - cue impromptu research on 'headbutting in goats' and sigh of relief as we find that its normal behaviour.

As if goat ownership in itself weren't enough excitement, we also had unforeseen shenanigans with our crooked old sheds due to the impromptu increase in goats and the knock-on impact that it had on our other animals. We decided when we just had Goat that we were uncomfortable having her in an outdoor paddock all night, particularly when the bad weather inevitably hits, and so we relocated our bikes and turned the bike shed into a goat shed, with straw on the floor for warmth, a big water bucket and a feed trough nailed to a convenient post. But this goat shed was a single berth and totally unsuitable for both Cow and Goat together, regardless of how well they got on, so we turned our large rabbit shed into a goat shed and the small goat shed into a rabbit shed. Sorted! The morning routine that developed from here on was hugely enjoyable and not a million miles away from my idyllic daydreams. Just before sunrise, the chooks, bustling impatiently against their shed hatch, were let out into their run and had their grain refilled; the tarp on the front of the rabbit shed was rolled up and secured as they ran over to greet the morning light and dried corn cobs thrown down for them; and all water bowls were tipped out and refreshed. But what gave us the most pleasure was our new task - the milking. Goat and Cow were milked at dawn in the porch of their shed, after which they were led to the paddock area where they spent all their daytime hours, then taken back to the shed just before dusk for a second milking, a scratch on the nose and bed.

Before milking we'd prepare warm water and an old flannel to wash their udders and a few cups of grain for them to munch on to keep them occupied and still. They were tethered one at a time in the shed for milking and again separately at night for extra security but when in the paddock they were free to move about as they pleased, which included scratching their flanks against the sagging fence, lying sleepily in the sunshine and, of course, Cow would be on her tree stump. We milked into a clean metal bucket, and both Joe and I quickly improved with daily practice to be just as efficient as the previous owner. Although Cow filled most of the bucket, we persisted with Goat for the sake of good routine and when finished we took the milk to the kitchen, strained it through a muslin cloth and cooled it as quickly as possible in sterilised jars in the pantry. Even with no fridge, this process was fairly easy in the cooler autumnal months and we had little spoilage unless you count when Cow kicked the bucket and we lost a litre onto the floor ... but there's no point crying over spilt milk! We now had the novelty of being able to provide our own milk for tea and coffee, our porridge and muesli. We made yoghurt and milkshakes, flavouring them with our own fruit jams. And we made soft cheese, using lemon juice to curdle the milk and hanging the curds in muslin cloth from the ceiling beam to drain from the whey. In the spirit of wasting nothing, the whey was used as the liquid in our bread making, mixed with the chicken's feed for extra protein and was an effective face mask and psoriasis treatment when mixed some with oatmeal. Having our own milk was a revelation for us - it felt like it completed the homestead.

Our chickens had arrived at the end of the previous winter and were well established by the autumn, although a little diminished in number. We originally bought ten hens and rooster from a nearby village and drove them home snuggled in our large dog cage, where the hens huddled so closely together it looked like we were transporting a giant feather blanket. The huge rooster was transported separately in a cardboard box, which he was not happy about and tried to kick his way out of the whole journey home. We released them together into the shed that we had prepared over the previous months with a roost and some perches made from scraps of wooden pallets. We'd also wind proofed the shed with plastic removals packaging and spread some straw about the floor and roost for warmth and comfort against the biting winter cold, which was only just subsiding at that time. Through a small hatch at the back of their shed, they had access to an outside run that was fenced off to protect them from the dog and to protect our crops from them. We had become more attached to our chooks than expected and like to think that they grew to like us too - they had such charming characters, running up to us at the fence when we came to them with kitchen scraps and running back into the shed again when any small aircraft flew a little too low for their liking, as if the sky were about to fall. Autumn was great for them because the crops were dwindling and we could risk letting them loose in the garden where they accompanied us in our work, whether it be garden chores or simply washing the dishes. They would fuss about, pecking up insects and sounding like they were playing little trumpets at our feet with gentle, tuneful parps, occasionally veering off to the safety of their shed in a fluster of feathers if Penfold got too close. Then there were the eggs - huge, fresh, bright-yolked and delicious. We bought special feed for our birds, baked and ground their shells into their feed if their shells were ever soft and even went into their run and dug up worms for them from time to time as a treat. We never had an abundance of eggs considering the number of hens we had, but there was always enough and we were content in knowing that there were no cruel cages involved. They had originated from dubious conditions and had slightly stunted, misshapen beaks which we found later may have been due to beak cropping at a young age to stop them pecking at each other, as many industrial egg producers do, so we were keen to provide them with a happy home in return for a few fresh eggs. Their shed was cleaned out weekly, but despite making sure that the chickens were well cared for we still had lots of sudden deaths. We lost the rooster after just a week which wasn't a huge surprise given that he always seemed too heavy for his own legs. We suspect that the night he died, he had face planted onto the cold concrete floor and couldn't get himself up again. We had a big discussion about whether or not to eat him, not knowing how exactly he had died, together with the fact that he couldn't be bled out properly through the killing process meant that even if the meat was safe to eat, it would likely be tough and unpalatable. However, we'd never prepared a bird for the table before, so Joe respectfully donned his roast chicken shaped woolly hat and we went through the process of plucking and butchering the bird, for educational purposes only. We cracked out our new brazier and got a fire started to heat a big vat of water, in which we dipped the dead rooster to help loosen the feathers for plucking, which was difficult at first but got easier with practise and he soon started looking less like a wet bird and more like something you might find in the supermarket. The butchery was a bit harder, perhaps because we didn't have the perfect knife. Joe cut off the feet with a knife and some brute force, took the head off with an axe ... and then like true novices, we ran inside to consult our self-sufficiency book about how to get the insides on the outside. A bit of slicing and muckiness later involving hands submerged in chicken cavity, we had a quite neatly butchered bird, but one a hell of a lot slimmer than we had expected given his size and strength with his feathers on. We both looked at each other, then looked down into the bucket of chicken limbs, entrails and feathers, looked at each other again, then agreed to bury everything underneath the fire pit, not even wanting to risk Penfold's health with any unknown diseases. The dog may well have disagreed, but was fortunately very well behaved throughout the whole process, showing a keen interest but certainly no canine bloodlust. All in all, it was the educational experience we hoped it would be. Back to the hen-house, with no chance of chicks, we decided that we likely wouldn't be eating any of the remaining birds. But over the following months, several of the hens were fine one night, cold and stiff the next morning, good for nothing but to be buried on the outskirts of the garden (without any further butchery training). We learned that this could be quite common, but it didn't make it any easier. There was a glimmer of failure there, but we put it down to experience and tried to remain positive.

Our young rabbits, intended for breeding as meat, had joined us in the spring. They were bought from a big animal market with Sandor, who on spotting a bargain, saw fit to add to our two female and one male with three further unsexed bunnies who turned out to be a breed called 'Flemish giant' or something equally terrifying - just until he had constructed a hutch of his own. After some extensive internet research, we had settled on a pretty unconventional set up that suited our needs, our finances and our wish to keep our animals in as pleasant an environment as possible - we hated the idea of animals in cages with separate water bottles and forced mating. We, therefore, prepared a communal shed for them with concrete floor to prevent burrowing, a frontage constructed of pallets and chicken wire, a raised nesting box with two compartments, plenty of hay flooring and shared bowls for water and feed. This allowed the rabbits to socialise, mate, run around a little and huddle together for warmth. The shed had no solid front wall and so the bunnies had plenty of morning sun through the chicken wire in which they stretched out and they generally seemed pretty content, particularly when they started to get their share of kitchen scraps brought to them on a regular basis. For a few months we'd been watching the rabbits growing gradually larger, and they were just beginning to show signs of canoodling, but so far they chose only to use the nesting boxes as their primary toilet area rather than birthing a much-antici-pated litter. They were never named due to their likely demise, but we still did grow attached to them. They were cute as you might expect, but also quite smart and brassy. The smaller of them managed to escape several times, never running away but sitting on the wrong side of the fence eating tufts of grass calmly as if to say 'why bother?' and none of them showed any fear whatsoever of the curious dog who regularly stuck his snout against the chicken wire to get a good whiff of them. They merely sniffed him back, literally nose to nose, and went about the business of chewing dried corn from the cobs. On the arrival of the goats, we managed to main-tain the communal shed arrangement for the rabbits in the smaller shed, made much easier by Sandor having reclaimed his three super-sized bunnies after we threatened to have them for dinner. He promised that he'd still share the meat when he butchered them, but thought they'd have a few more months of growth in them ... if he's right then we estimated that they'd be the size of baby rhinos by Christmas.

*****

October brought with it a smattering of wind, rain and the first single-digit nighttime temperatures in a long time. It brought the winter duvet out of hibernation and the merino jumpers and thermals out of their boxes under the bed, making space for the shorts that were packed away for another year. Both the kitchen and bedroom fires were tested for birds nests and other blockages, although there had only been an occasional need for them to take the edge off the cooler nights as the house tended to stay quite cosy, insulated as it was by its thick mud walls. Penfold returned to his favourite cool weather residence under the duvet while the outdoor cats tried their best to become indoor cats. And the last cricket that had chirruped prettily outside the bedroom window through the summer nights finally vacated the pear tree for another year ... either that or we could simply no longer hear him anymore as the windows were now all firmly closed.

By the time a new season is about to hit, Joe and I are usually looking forward to a change of pace, the different smells in the air and colours in the trees. But we absolutely love autumn. You can almost feel the garden winding down, breathing deeper and relaxing after busying itself for so long over spring and sweating it out all summer. We go into harvest mode, collecting goodies that won't like the impending frostiness, leaving only the hardy veg that can remain in the ground through to winter - the savoy cabbages, chard, kale, leeks and parsnips. Carrots are dug up and packed in buckets of cool moist sand, potatoes are gathered and kept in sacks on the cold pantry floor, the courgette, pepper and tomato plants are pulled up and thrown on the compost now that their fruits have diminished; the green tomatoes remaining are either pickled or left in the pantry to slowly ripen. Any orange tinged squash are collected and arranged on the porch to finish ripening and cure in the sun and chillies are threaded onto string and hung under the roof overhang to dry. We're lucky enough to get a large bucket of green chillies from Tamas and Margit, so we'll spend a day or two, pickling some, fermenting some for hot sauce and chargrilling the rest for making a lovely smokey chipotle sauce. The herbs are trimmed back and bunches pegged out with the chilli garlands. Tight bunches of black grapes are cut and pressed in our small manual fruit press, providing several litres of rich perfumed grape must, so sticky sweet that we need to water it down to drink. Windfall apples are collected and kept in buckets in the shade for casual al fresco chomping or spontaneous pies and crumbles. In fact, the only downside that we can find about this time of the year is the sudden fruit fly infestation, we presume encouraged by the ripening fruit on the vines outside our windows and decomposing windfall under the trees around the garden. The critters float around the windows in busy clouds, unable to be swatted as any motion simply wafts them around the room for them to reconvene back at the window in seconds where they make the house feel dirty and our skin crawl. Our only solution has been fly-traps made from cider vinegar in old jars and a little patience, which works well enough. Now's also the time that we throw down some grass seed to continue thickening our lawn, get onion sets and garlic bulbs in the ground for next years crop and plant any trees and shrubs that we feel the garden might benefit from. This October was the addition of a lovely little hazel sapling at the bottom of the garden, which when it matures a little, will provide us with increased soil structure in a soggy area of the lawn, additional leafy privacy from our neighbour, hazelnuts and pretty catkins through winter.

The plots empty as the now fruitless plants are pulled up and the weeds begin to brown off and recede, showing bare earth again for the first time in months. And this is when we take up our forks and start to dig over the garden, to remove weeds and incorporate some of our home produced compost. We progress plot by plot, not in any rush as we have the next few months to get the work complete, and besides, this autumn was not a patch on our first year when the garden was still overgrown and overrun with an assortment of huge and invasive weeds. Taking the work steadily prevents what some might consider inevitable back injuries and ensures that it remains enjoyable - we love that its cool enough to get back to some physical work again, it gets the blood pumping and gives us good reason to be out breathing fresh air, noticing the flocks of migrating geese in formation overhead and myriad of weird and wonderful mini-creatures living in and on the soil. Of course, this work is all done under the watchful eyes of Goat and Cow, always on the lookout for a tasty treat from the weed bucket and more than happy to sing, very loudly, for their supper. We're often accompanied by our hens, who on seeing the procession of human, fork and bucket making their way to an empty plot, follow us faithfully and all simultaneously try to fulfil some bizarre death wish by placing their little heads underneath the descending fork prongs at any given opportunity. We've had no fork related chicken deaths, but the numbers continued to dwindle, leaving us with seven in total - five of our original crooked beaked beauties and two new, large glamorous hens, bought by Joe's mum from the animal market on her last visit out to see us. To add insult to injury, Joe has accidentally, but on more than one occasion, dug up one of our buried chickens while turning over the veg plots, scaring himself half to death when a clawed foot sprung out at him from the soil. I guess it should have taught him to bury them deeper in the ground, but he never did. I wondered briefly, leaning on my fork, what it would be like if these buried birds actually sprouted and grew into fully fledged poultry trees, from which we could pick our own eggs, chicken breast fillets and thighs ... until the continuous peck, peck, pecking on my wellington boot brought me back round to the job at hand. There was a glimmer of hope with the chooks though, that came in the unlikely form of an armful of crawling mites following a standard roost clean and a pot of 'chicken dust'. It turned out, after some research, that these lice could make the chickens sick, consequently preventing them from laying and could quite easily be the cause of their sudden deaths. We made a dry dirt-bath box for them to use and bought some mite treatment powder from our local pet store, which was sprinkled liberally around their roosting area every week, while we waited hopefully for the creepy crawlies to abate and the remaining chickens to survive.

The digging did not stop at just preparing our land for next year's crops, but also this year involved digging a couple of root cellars adjacent to the goat pen. Joe's innovation involved sinking a couple of our huge cracked water butts into the ground, connecting some hose-pipe tubing for ventilation, insulating with a thick layer of straw and then covering with a hatch constructed from a lined pallet and some of the thinner logs from our mammoth wood delivery the previous year. Many rural homes in Hungary come with multiple outhouses, a well and an underground cellar. Although we had the sheds, we had no well or cellar, both of which would have been a real boon considering our simple way of life. The cellars, in particular, are designed to be just deep enough to stay at a constant temperature - cool in summer and cool, but not freezing in winter. A great place to store your excess vegetables through autumn and winter, or barrels of wine if you happened to have them. Root cellars work along the same lines on a smaller scale, although not as deep as the cellar and therefore less reliable in extremes of temperature. Nevertheless, our cellars were tested out with a thermometer for a week or so, before being loaded up with sacks of beetroot, squash and a collection of large jars with various fruity or pickled contents. We planned to check on the stash fairly regularly and remained open-minded about its success seeing as we'd spent nothing on them, other than some of Joe's elbow grease.

*****

October marked the start of our autumnal foraging which was easily and surreptitiously incorporated into our daily dog-walks. We'd go out with empty pockets and a few extra dog-poo bags and return with a haul of hawthorn or sloe berries, rosehips, oyster mushrooms and walnuts. Bags and bags of walnuts. No walk was complete without at least a handful secreted about various pockets - the trees seemed to line every road and path in the village. It was an addictive activity too, walnut collection. On a good day, perhaps following a gale or storm that dislodged a good quantity of nuts, we could find ourselves bent over and fixated on the ground in a greedy trance because once you get your eye in, they seem to all come out of hiding and there are nuts everywhere. Each year we'd gradually gather several kilos and hang them to dry in old potato net sacking under the porch, to ensure that they would last through the year.

Autumn is a great time for dog walks for several reasons, aside from the foraging and the beautiful smells of wood smoke and fermenting apples on overloaded trees. It's a bustling time in the fields on the outskirts of the village as the harvests begin in earnest, especially along the pretty vineyard-lined paths that lead through to the open cornfields beyond. Families and friends all club together and help with the grape harvest, grafting all day, stopping only for a bowl of steaming goulash served from a huge vat hung from a tripod over a fire. If we time our morning or evening walk just right we can be offered regular tastes of freshly pressed sweet grape must or even a sample of last year's wine from several locals, all more than happy to show off their wares and take you on a tour of their cellars. Most villages put on some form of harvest festival to mark the season too, there are themed decorations, alarming stuffed scarecrows positioned at the side of roads and in our village there is a parade, with dancing in traditional costume, horses with garlanded carts and a uniformed horseman cracking an impossibly long whip, guaranteed to panic Penfold into the nearest flowerbed. And while the quaint and traditional takes place in the village streets, out in the vast fields there are monstrous machines with colossal wheels and giant teeth chewing their way through acre upon acre of corn and sunflowers.

Most of the larger fields well outside of the village belong to large conglomerates who harvest on a monumental scale, but the land immediately surrounding us tends to be owned by locals who each have a couple of acres of land at their disposal, normally in long strips leading back from their house or a small cellar building on the vineyard tracks. It's one of these that Sandor had asked if we'd like to help him with one sunny weekend. On the Saturday afternoon, after Penfold had been walked, all daily chores completed and the goats well secured, he picked us up in one of his old dilapidated tractors, complete with an intimidating and rickety cutting attachment. With Joe and I perched either side of Sandor high up in the cab, pressed against the glass, we took a bone-crushing, bum-numbing but hugely fun trip up to his fields at the back of the village, feeling like excited kids. We collected scraps of sunflower heads from his neighbour's already ploughed field and gathered more walnuts. Then Joe and I would each take a big bucket and disappear for 15 minutes at a time into the prickly undergrowth, popping the corn cobs out of their husks so that the leaves were left on the stems for bundling up later, while Sandor drove after us in the tractor, cutting the plants and ensuring that we kept up a good pace. After a few hours of hard graft we had sore hands from the prickly sunflower heads and aching wrists from the repetitive corn picking but were satisfied with a few big sacks of corn cobs and an empty field, so it came as a bit of a surprise when Sandor pointed to another stretch of land across the track. Perhaps noticing our crestfallen faces, he declared that he had brought a packed lunch for us so we had a break and chatted for a while. Quickly rejuvenated, we dutifully continued but convinced Sandor to stop for the day by the time we had seven big sacks full of corn, a sack of sunflower heads and a large bucket of walnuts, realising that we would probably all be travelling in the same tractor cab together. The journey home was a farce. The doors took several attempts to get securely closed and Joe had to lift a sack of corn every time Sandor needed to change gear. Or brake. He couldn't see out of any window other than the front and calmly told us that we'd probably get in trouble with the police if they saw us travelling like this. It was all worth it though, as when we pulled up onto our driveway, much to Tamas' amusement next door, all of the sacks of goodies were unloaded and given to us to take in for our animals. The following day we decided to skip the tractor ride and met Sandor up at his field to finish off picking the corn, while he faffed around setting fire to rows of dry, cut corn stems, as is fairly normal practice if the plumes of smoke and charred ground in other fields is anything to go by. The wind was whipping up a bit, but we noticed that Sandor wasn't too concerned when his neighbour's corn started to go up in smoke ... and to be fair I wasn't overly worried as it would cover the fact that I had accidentally been picking the wrong corn for half an hour the previous day, before he bothered to explain where the boundaries were. Apart from the obvious benefits of sacks of animal feed and the occasional picnic basket of bread, greasy pieces of fried duck and fizzy drinks prepared by Sandor's' wife, we loved the feeling created through lending our time in return for his ongoing support. Way better than working in an office to make money to buy the animal feed, why not help to gather the animal feed directly?! It was great being out of the house, out in the community, exchanging goods for services with no cash changing hands. And all this fun and games to the backdrop of a harvest festival fun fayre back in the village, where the loud bass started thumping at 9 am despite the fact that no-one was yet there.

Kale & Walnut Pesto

When the kale is good to go and the walnuts are starting to drop themselves with gay abandon we throw the two together for this quick and easy pesto that can be used as a topping for thick crusty toast or stirred into your favourite pasta. The added bonus is that it's super nutritious!

ingredients:
kale
walnuts
juice of half a lemon (or a few squirts of bottled lemon juice)
a generous glug of vegetable/olive oil
salt and pepper

Wash the kale, cut out the thick stems and chop roughly. Put the kale and all the other ingredients into a blender and blitz into a smooth paste. Add more oil/lemon juice if the consistency is too thick for your liking and add salt and pepper to taste. Spoon into small sterilised jars. Kept in a cool place these jars of pesto should keep for several months.

CHAPTER FIVE

November 2015

Not built like a brick shithouse

"So, uuuuum, where does the, um, where does the poo go?" I had asked Eniko, back in February, when we were taking a first look at our bathroom-to-be.

"It all goes outside" was the confident but unhelpful response as she waved her hand dismissively at the pipes leading into the thick walls.

"But, I mean, is it connected to mains sewage or is there a cesspit?"

"Because the house isn't on the road, it must go into the garden"

Joe and I glanced at each other quizzically, both of us assuming that she didn't mean to be taken literally. We tried a few more questions, but getting nowhere, mentally logged it under one of the few 'cons' of this particular property and moved on to mooching around the rest of the house.

I understand that it's not normal to spend a lot of

time discussing toilets and their innermost workings. But the thing is, you only realise how important they are if you don't have one. Or if you do have one but don't know where they empty out to and face the potentially stinky repercussions of blockages and overflows. I would imagine it's not the best way to endear yourself to new neighbours. We never really got to the bottom of the situation and to this day have a little nervousness about where the indoor toilet actually flushes out to. There were no house plans made available and nobody seemed to have any concrete answers, but we considered our 75p monthly bill from the water company confirmation enough of not being connected to any mains waste system. By November we had cleared our way to all corners of our land and there were no signs of any hatches, pits or concrete tanks that could indicate a sunken cesspit. The closest we had got was a suspicious looking piece of old hose pipe protruding from the ground between two apple trees at the very bottom of the garden, which we didn't touch for months in case it had some important but unknown use. The pipe was carefully pulled up eventually as part of Joe's landscaping of the lower garden behind the house that autumn and fortunately nothing, to our knowledge anyway, has happened as a consequence. It was just a piece of discarded hosepipe. He was at the time manually creating a couple of terraces to level out the slope there and it was then that we found some clues to our sewage arrangements. His spade hit something large and concrete about two feet deep, not too far from the corner of the house where the bathroom was located. We didn't bother excavating fully, but it was clear that if this was the tank, there was no hatch by which the contents could be emptied. We came to the conclusion that we indeed had a septic tank, likely a 'soakaway', meaning that the liquid contents could slowly leach from it and we would not have the cost or inconvenience of having to have it emptied regularly. The good news was that we'd been using the indoor toilet for several months with no problem, there were no unwanted aromas either inside or outside of the house that suggested anything was amiss. But we still weren't comfortable with our set up. The indoor loo was a standard western toilet bowl, but it had no cistern, just a pipe with a small stopcock that controlled a stream of water for flushing. This was fine for the most part, but it couldn't handle paper well and 'number twos' required a turbo flush that could only be provided by a bucket of rainwater that sat next to the toilet. We worried about toilet paper clogging the tank up, were concerned at not knowing the size of the tank and didn't like the idea of chemical cleaning products potentially seeping into the soil, no matter where it emptied out. This was the uneasy arrangement that turned our attention to the small brick toilet building that sat discreetly crumbling behind our row of sheds.

It was early in November and the trees were beginning to look a little bare. The ground was becoming brown and emptying as our weeding progressed and new growth slowed to a halt. It was a fairly standard autumnal day; early-on a cold, heavy fog shrouded the garden preventing any visibility much past the sheds and certainly not beyond the garden boundaries, but this more often than not burned off to a pleasantly mild, sunny day. We waited for the sun to do its work and by mid-morning were both standing under a blue sky, examining our outdoor loo, which we had condemned and declared out of bounds four months earlier due to the rotten wooden floor, seat and walls. There was no way it could be used in its current condition - we couldn't even make the floor safe while the brick shed stood over it as the pit plunged into deep darkness straight down from the walls. It had to be dismantled, then we could consider how to create an alternative which we so desperately needed to take the pressure off our weedy little indoor loo, with its questionable sewage system.

"So, how are we going about this?" Joe asked, heavy lump-hammer in hand. He'd already wrenched the green painted wooden door from its frame and crow-barred the flaking, spongy floorboards and toilet structure out of the building with minimal wreckage falling into the valuable pit space. Together, with the help of a ladder, we had carefully lifted off the tiles from the roof and the wooden frame that had held them there. We were left with the concrete coated brick structure, surrounding an intimidating looking hole of nearly four feet in diameter. "You've got to hit it from the inside - we don't want to fill the pit with bricks. And we might want the bricks for something later anyway." I replied. Joe cautiously mounted the ladder, held on to the back wall, dangled his arm and hammer over the pit and took a decent swing at a side wall. Bricks fell from the top of the wall, cartoon-like cracks spread across the concrete and the wall took on a new bowed shape. "I think that might do it actually," Joe said as he re-positioned himself and gave the wall a shove. In slow motion, the wall flopped and folded outwards into a pile, concrete splintering as it hit the floor in a cloud of dust. It turns out that our brick shit-house was not, in fact, built like one. The rest of the walls were pushed over just as easily. We retrieved the bricks, tidied the rubble into a pile and made safe the gaping hole by covering it with the toilet door and old wooden planks from the sheds - we didn't want our pit being filled with careless hedgehogs ... or dogs.

Both Joe and I, when looking into living a more

simple life, were keen on off-grid options and so having a long-drop or composting toilet really appealed to us. Even though we'd just razed our outdoor loo to the ground, the most important part was still intact - the hole. We were chuffed with our hole. It would have taken a lot of time and effort to dig something that large and deep by ourselves, plus it seemed sturdy and was in a good position - tucked to the rear of our row of sheds and accessible from the main house by a concrete path. It was private enough that in the lushness of summer, one could leave the door wide open and partake in peaceful, al fresco number twos in the morning sunshine, a simple pleasure that should never be poo-pooed.

The problem now was rebuilding another appropriate structure over the hole. We stood staring for hours at the space where the toilet shed once stood, scratching our chins, racking our brains, testing and teasing options that might be safe and suitable. We knew that we had to create some sort of floor area around the pit, no matter how large the toilet structure ended up being, so we spent some time at our local builder's yard and came home with four ridiculously heavy reinforced concrete beams to lay across the top of the pit. They were cemented into place with even gaps between them, enough to allow for a toilet to be positioned on or above them with an unobstructed access area into the hole for obvious reasons. Now, back to the original dilemma of what structure to house our loo. A garden shed with a wooden bench? A porcelain loo on a wooden floor? Rebuild the brick shed, but bigger and stronger? All options seemed to be excessively difficult and way too expensive for us. Then we tapped into the one resource that we knew wouldn't let us down - our friend Sandor. Within a week he had found a supplier of ready-made wooden outhouses online, complete with bench seat, lid and floor for a reasonably priced £100. Unfortunately though, they were based nearly two hours drive away on the wrong side of Budapest and didn't deliver.

Operation 'long-drop' was never going to be as simple as it should have been, partly because we were in Hungary rather than the UK, and partly because we had involved Sandor, who, for all his help and enthusiasm, was prone to over-complicating even the most simple of tasks. We had to collect the toilet ourselves and with no tow-bar or roof-rack on our own car, the three of us were having to take a trip to Budapest in Sandor's battered old Ford Focus that had seen several accidents and several subsequent DIY repair jobs. We drove to Budapest on pot-holed back roads to avoid a toll charge for the highway, making a couple of unplanned stops in seedy-looking suburbs for Sandor to pick up random online bargains - "We just stop here for a moment, let's see, I think this is the man. I have bought many VHS videos at a good price. No-one buys VHS vidcos now. Only me". We reached the timber yard and warehouse later than we would have liked, but once there paid our money and made use of several big, burly men to get the wooden shed strapped securely to the car. The journey home involved getting stuck in Budapest rush-hour and some strong winds and hasty braking that made Joe and I outwardly cringe as we expected the toilet to jolt from its fastenings and crash forward onto the bonnet of the car. We had previously agreed with Sandor to stop off at the county hospital on our way home so that he could briefly tend to his sick 'father-in-love', so he dropped us off at a nearby supermarket to grab some much-needed snacks. It wasn't until we were waiting outside for Sandor's return, in the now cold evening air, that we saw a vehicle turn into the car park with a ridiculously large wooden box lashed to its roof and realised just how much like a Mr Bean film this trip had been. Nevertheless we made it home in one piece and somehow, in the dark, Joe and Sandor managed to manhandle the shed from the car roof to the concrete path just outside our house, where it remained, a hulking shadow in the slowly descending fog, waiting patiently for some wood stain and someone strong enough to help Joe lift it into place.

That someone came in the shape of Joe's dad, during his parent's first visit to our fledgeling homestead. Their visit also gave the newly positioned toilet a proper initiation, used by four people daily over the course of a long weekend. Its performance was exemplary - it took number twos, toilet paper and a handful of sawdust to help decomposition, felt sturdy and did not emit a single undesirable odour. The only minor inconvenience was the fact that the loo had to be a wee-free zone, so as to keep it smelling fresh; something that was not always easy but was mastered with practice and the appropriate preparation! It was declared a success and saved the indoor toilet from the likely hazardous blockages of overuse.

Over the following week, as Joe took up his spade and returned to levelling the back of the garden into a terrace, I took up various pots of wood stain, paint and varnish and set about protecting our new loo from the elements. It was stained a dark green that camouflaged it nicely into the surrounding undergrowth and after the interior was painted and varnished I finished the floor with a few tiles and hung some solar fairy lights around the top. The loo was equipped with a waterproof bag full of toilet paper, a tin full of sawdust and a small dustpan-brush for keeping everything tidy, that doubled up as a tool to sweep around the loo rim for any uninvited visitors. The toilet has remained fresh as a daisy, dry, clean and I've actually seen less creepy crawlies in there than any indoor bathroom. The only hitch in the very early stages was when Joe used it a day or so after my paint job. It was the crack of dawn when he came in from the garden and asked for my help, backing up to me slowly and dropping his jeans - a ring of bright yellow gloss paint perfectly circled his buttocks. It's not every morning you spend attending to your partner's paint covered bum cheeks with a white-spirit soaked rag!

*****

Towards the end of November there's a seasonal gear shift that we have the time to really savour; This is partly because after months of warmth we're ready for a change (and those changes seem quite pronounced in Hungary) but also because we were becoming far more absorbed in our environment. We noticed the catkins developing on hazel trees, the rich assorted hues of the Rhus leaves and the contrast between the dark skeletal hedgerows and their glossy scarlet berries. There's a smell of wood fires in the air and at first light chimneys throughout the village start to puff out their smoke signals, letting everyone know that their inhabitants are awake. In the fields on the outskirts of the village, now that the tall corn and sunflowers have been harvested, the bare fields look as if they go on forever and there's a beautiful bleakness like the expanse of an empty beach in winter. I hadn't appreciated this desolate landscape on our initial visits here, but now we were living amongst it, aware of the nuances, watching it morph into something different from month to month, it felt good. It felt like a rite of passage, seeing through the darker days so as to be rewarded with a beautiful spring and a bountiful summer. And as if to counterbalance the gloom, heavy crystalline frosts became more regular, decorating everything in the garden. Even the dirty dishes left out overnight freeze to the table and look stunning, sugar-coated and glimmering.

Despite Halloween not being a huge event in Hungary, villager's gardens are commonly adorned with carved pumpkins, candles and decorations during autumn. This seems to be a simple nod to the recently finished harvests, rather than the Americanised traditions of dressing up and trick or treating, although there could be the beginnings of a shift if the larger shops and supermarkets get their way. What is celebrated though is All Saints and All Souls days. Cemeteries, found on the outskirts of every village, are well tended and colourful all year round, but in November are lit throughout with ornate glass jars containing flickering candles. It's a beautiful and quite ethereal sight, guaranteed to move even the most steadfastly cynical of people.

With a few extra layers of clothing, work in the garden continued - the fruit trees were pruned back, the grapevines were mounded up with

carth to protcct thcm from thc harsh tempera
tures due over the coming months and chainsawing was taken up in earnest with the help, at
different times, of Sandor and Tamas. Both had
very relaxed approaches to this highly risky
task, there were no gloves or protective glasses
used and certainly no chaps to cover the legs. I
was always incredibly paranoid around the
chainsawing activity, probably heightened because of the accident rehabilitation work that I
used to do in New Zealand, talking to guys who
had sunk the saws into their thighs or had the
machines kickback into their arms and faces.
Watching Sandor secure a huge log with his foot,
protected only by a battered plastic Crocs clog,
was enough to make me very fidgety, but he'd
work for hours comfortably like this, reducing
our huge log pile into choppable hunks ready for
axing. I was always a little more confident with
Tamas, because although he didn't have the protective gear either, always had a cigarette stuck
to his lips and was the smaller of the two men, he
was more certain and steady in his technique -
there were no precariously balanced branches or
questionable choices in how the chainsaw was
directed. But Tamas was a machine. He would
have worked from 9 am through to nightfall
with just a 10-minute lunch break given the
chance. One morning, Joe had cracked out the
chainsaw to chop up just a few logs, but was well
and truly hijacked by Tamas spotting what he

was up to through the bare hedgerow and wanting to help out. What began with 'a few' logs turned into 'all the remaining logs' over several days, a very full woodshed and a small mountain of wood chippings. The two of them sawed through a massive pile of logs that day and we were very happy that we could move the wood into the shed rather than it gathering moisture and mould under the increasingly brittle and holey tarpaulins. Tamas seemed content with his help and the home-made beer (declared 'prima' - first rate) that we plied him with, saying that he would help saw some more next year. The following day Tamas was around again to chainsaw some more wood, despite it not being 'next year' yet. We didn't have the heart (or the vocabulary) to turn him away, so more logs were sawn and more wood chippings created, great for the composting loo. This happened again the day after, by which time we had fortunately run out of the outdoor log piles to saw, so the job should have been finished, with a good three years worth of wood ready in the shed. Joe tried his best to cover the fact that we had more logs in another shed, but failed miserably and we spent a good 10 minutes telling him that it's OK, we had enough and we don't need it cut. I think he just liked playing with our chainsaw. And we also think he said something along the lines of "what else are you going to do, go back to bed?".

It was with this help though, that we were left with sheds full of prepared firewood and finally felt set up for the coming winter. On a daily basis, Joe would continue to chop the chain-sawed logs with a hefty axe into wood small enough to fit our wood burners, while I went back to the last few patches of garden that needed weeding. The battle of the bindweed was in full force again. Despite its pretty pastel flowers in summer, it really has the most horrible roots that twisted deeply through every inch of our veggie-plots-to-be. Apparently, it's known as 'devil's guts' which is pretty appropriate given its evilness and that sometimes a nice long stretch of the stuff can be dug up in one go, springing out of the soil and coiling up like intestines. Those occasions are hugely satisfying, but more often than not it snaps in several places and hides back in the ground, ready to multiply the following year.

Our house was by this time more or less the finished article on the inside at least, simple but warm and homely, just in time to snuggle away from the longer, colder nights. All rooms were painted and decorated and we had found appropriate cupboards and shelves to kit out our kitchen without having to resort to fitted furniture which would have looked completely out of place. We'd bought a wood fire stove for the kitchen too, from a Hungarian English teacher who, Sandor said, refused to believe that we were from England because our accents were apparently so unconvincing and our language skills so poor. The wood burner heated the kitchen quickly and although it couldn't hold the heat like our big ceramic bedroom fire, we used the cast iron surface for cooking and were always sure to have a full kettle of water on the boil for numerous cups of tea to warm our cockles throughout the day. Our lack of appliances was not causing us any great problem either. We continued to wash dishes in the garden, hang our laundry out on sunnier days and take our rugs outside for vigorous shaking in the absence of a vacuum cleaner. It certainly took more time, but we were currently blessed with plenty of that. We remained fridge-less, still using our little terracotta creation in the pantry for dairy and occasional meat purchases, but through autumn the pantry itself was pretty much perfect fridge temperature anyway. In the bathroom, Joe had successfully plumbed in a bathtub which ended up being the perfect size for our relatively small 50-litre water heater. We had considered upgrading to a larger one, but actually, as we were in the habit of sharing our bathwater we felt that it would have been an unnecessary cost. The only downside to our bathroom was that it was the coldest room of the house, but I tried to justify the situation by telling myself that it was as recently as my parent's childhood that outdoor loos were still common and ice formed inside the windows in a harsh winter. It wasn't all that bad - a toilet trip was only brief after all and certainly not as fresh as using our long-drop, and bath-times made the room fairly warm and steamy, so together with the after-bath glow, the room was bearable. And the bedroom was always toasty once we'd learned to start the fire early enough for its ceramic bulk to heat through.

It was during the longer nights and increased time inside the house that we decided our Hungarian language skills needed some serious attention. We had spent the four or five months while we were settling in familiarising ourselves with some very basic vocabulary, numbers and greetings for example, but we had really found it tough getting our heads around the 44 letters of the alphabet and the peculiar pronunciation of some letters. We used practised phrases in the post office when we took our paying-in chits to pay our bills, and we engaged our neighbours in some rehearsed small talk, but we always had trouble being fully understood. We'd generate smirks or puzzled expressions at almost every attempt and Tamas, next door, would talk at us incessantly. We could understand just enough to know that he was repeating the same thing at us in several different ways. On one occasion, when Sandor happened to be with us, we listened to a particularly long barrage of a convoluted mono-

logue from Tamas only to discover on transla-
tion that he had offered to help us paint the
exterior of our house in spring. Ten minutes of
speech was reduced to a simple sentence, which
didn't help much with the early stages of our
learning. But still, we persevered. In the bakery, the young staff member had become accustomed to us and knew our usual order, but she
still listened to our request of "Please, bread. Big
white can I have. Thank you." without too much
giggling and even corrected us once to help us
out. We knew that we had to improve though,
so we searched online and found videos, games,
quizzes and courses to help us on our way. We
would have plenty of time over winter for learning and so made a quiet pledge to ourselves,
dedicating a little time every day to practising
the language so that we could make more of
an effort with the locals that we were becoming more familiar with. In fact, I think most
people in the village were getting used to us and
knew we were trying, even though the butchering of their language must have been comical.
By now we had changed our car registration and
had Hungarian plates for insurance purposes, so
we felt less conspicuous. And the fact that we
showed no signs of heading back to the UK even
with winter approaching set us apart from most
of the other ex-pats that came to Hungary for
the finer months and although nothing was specifically said, we sensed an acceptance and fa-

miliarity that we hadn't had before.

Apple Butter

In autumn, we often have more apples than we know what to do with. A bucket of windfall fruit sits in the shade on the porch for weeks, for snacking or to make pies, apple cake and crumbles. Before the heavy frosts set in, we pick the remaining apples from the trees, wrap them in paper and put them in the pantry for long term storage - we do lose a few to rot and fruit fly, but on the whole, they keep surprisingly well. When we tire of the baking and we're still left with kilos of slightly bruised, blemished or pest-nibbled fruit, we make apple butter. It's a way of using a fair few kilos at a time and ensuring that we're able to access that moreish sweet-spicy goodness throughout winter and well into the following year. This thick, aromatic spread has nothing whatsoever to do with dairy but rather is a sweet alternative to butter - delicious on toast, scones and pancakes or wherever you might use jam. We've also discovered that it comes in handy as an egg replacer when baking vegan cakes.

Ingredients:
apples (any variety)
water
cider or apple vinegar

sugar

cinnamon, cloves, allspice

lemon

Wash and quarter the apples - the peel and core all goes in for flavour, but the pectin in the core also helps with the set of the butter. Heat in a pan with enough water to cover the bottom of the pan and a cup of vinegar per large pan of apples. Cook for 30 mins or so, until soft. After this, pass the appley mush through a sieve to remove pips and skins, leaving you with a thick, golden apple puree. This can take some time and patience, but it's worth it! Add the apple puree back into the pan with half a cup of sugar per cup of apple, and add your preferred spices to taste. Cook this up again until thick, pour into clean, sterilised jars and label. Stored in a cool place, this should keep well for over a year.

CHAPTER SIX

December 2017

The Christmas dilemma

Old habits die hard, as they say. And Christmas habits I've found particularly difficult to kill off. This is partly because I do really enjoy Christmas and all it's nostalgic, tinsel-clad, booze-soaked festiveness, but I suspect its also partly because of those ingrained first world pressures to join the masses in their gift-buying, card-sending, family-visiting, party-attending, tree-decorating and all-round media encouraged overindulgence. It wasn't the change of country that had been the challenge - we'd experienced Christmases in Asia, Australia and New Zealand so knew how to adapt to being away from family and had found no problem swapping the traditional turkey and mulled wine for 'surf n turf' and cold beer - but it was rather the change of lifestyle that I found most problematic in Hungary. With our attempt to be as self-sufficient as possible and our choice to live simply and not rely on paid work, we decided that the expense and extravagance of Christmas would clearly not be sustainable and, in fact, would be completely at odds with our lifestyle throughout the rest of the year. We had to find alternatives, but it turned out that I didn't realise quite how institutionalised I had become until that first Christmas in Hungary when I had to refrain from buying Christmas presents, cards, decorations and the usual excessive amount of edible treats. I found our first festive season frustrating and mildly traumatic. Throughout December Joe spent far more time than he should have had to saying 'no' to me repeatedly as I held up decorated boxes of chocolates, fancy cheeses and various bottles of booze under his nose in the hope that something, just maybe, would be allowed into the shopping trolley. Fortunately though, what we lacked in money we more than made up with available time and ingenuity, and we learned from our first Christmas forward, that we can be quite creative when it comes to making something from virtually nothing and now have our festive season down pat.

The first signs of Christmas can be found later than we've become accustomed to, at the beginning of December, rather than the moment the giant Haribo trick or treat multi-packs and ghoul masks disappear from the shop shelves. Decorative wreaths can be seen appearing on gates and front doors, fairy lights adorn front garden shrubs and porches, and the odd battered looking Santa figurine can be seen climbing rope-ladders attached to the side of a house or two. In the village square, just around the corner from us, one of the towering evergreens is strung with lights and decorated by the local schoolkids with bundles of gift-wrapped boxes and homemade Christmas crackers; sometimes hung with precision, but more often thrown into the branches with reckless abandon. This haphazard approach ensures that only one fairly small area of the tree is decorated, but it has a homely feel and disguises the odd pizza box that's thrown in for good measure. Beneath the Christmas tree is the obligatory and slightly creepy village nativity scene, housed in a simple three sided shed constructed of dried corn stems. Every year, faceless mannequins of Joseph and Mary can be found in this shed, positioned either side of a cradle. They're accompanied by a life-size fabric sheep with pink puckered lips and long eyelashes, clearly an integral member of the nativity story and a religious icon that has become our favourite. The shops in larger towns are decorated, have Christmas goodies for sale and play some classic festive tunes, but it doesn't feel half as tacky, excessive or intrusive as in the high streets and malls of the UK and there's certainly no Slade or Wizzard playing on repeat. The village shops have nothing more than maybe a little tinsel around the till. And although this may seem rather tame, we did get our first flashing village street lights this year ... they extended only to about six or seven of the many lamp-posts down our long main street, but we appreciated the effort all the same.

The gradual village transformation brings some much-needed cheer to the darker days and empty gardens, and not wanting to be left behind we truffled out the old cardboard box of decorations from the loft that we had shipped from England. With no Christmas tree and no plans to buy one, the baubles were hung on the pear tree just outside the front door, tinsel balanced across shelves and picture frames, and fairy lights draped beneath the large beam in our bedroom. We cut snowflakes out of scrap white paper and attached them to the windows, made wreaths from rosemary and lavender cuttings tied with red ribbon and scavenged some twigs with ruby red berries to go in a vase in place of a tree. This year I channelled my innermost Blue Peter and made large paper mache baubles from newspaper strips pasted around small balloons with flour and water glue, which were dried, painted, varnished and hung around the house. Not only did they look beautiful, but they kept me occupied as the garden chores dried up and weather shooed us back indoors. As December progressed our home looked just as, if not more festive than we've ever had at previous Christmastimes and we've found that there's something so much more pleasing about home crafted, unique and natural decorations than the mass-produced, synthetic kitsch that we'd accumulated in the years before our move to Hungary. And to intensify my dose of festive preparations I would mull wine and bake ginger cookies to fill the air with spicy sweetness while listening to A Christmas Carol on audiobook for good measure.

With advent well underway and the house looking and smelling appropriately cheery, my thoughts turned to family and the annual dilemma of what to do about cards and presents for everyone. We'd never been extravagant with our gifts even when employed, but we had always bought something for everyone and certainly sent a big bundle of cards to friends and family around the world, which in itself is not particularly cheap. Despite Joe's protestations, I was adamant that cards had to be sent. I felt that it was the one time of year that was especially important to make some sort of connection with those we cared about, especially those who aren't so enamoured with social media. The compromise that we came to was that cards were sent to close friends and family, but emails and Facebook messages would be the best way forward with our other contacts. The next problem was the fact that Hungarians don't really do

Christmas cards. They're available but tend to be large elaborate and expensive single cards rather than the numerous glittery charity boxes that you can grab at BOGOF prices in most UK supermarkets, and therefore simply not an option for us. So in true self-sufficiency mode, I had a scrounge around the loft boxes and discovered some card, paper, envelopes and old Christmas cards that could be cut about and re-assembled as fairly passable craft-style cards that didn't look too embarrassing at all. The cost of postage was still higher than we would have liked, but I considered it worthwhile given that we were not spending much on the cards themselves, or presents to go with them. Yes, that's right. No presents. Well, that's not strictly true as I had allocated myself a £10 each budget for nieces and nephews at Christmas, but we'd discussed presents with our adult family and explained that it would not be an option buying gifts for everyone. It was very uncomfortable at first, particularly knowing that our families would no doubt continue to buy gifts for us, although I think the discomfort was largely down to societal pressure rather than a real need or desire for endless inane 'stuff'. I was pretty sure that my siblings would quite happily go without another pair of themed socks or gift boxed bath bubbles, but I felt like I wasn't playing along. There was the option of homemade gifts of course, but the cost of postage when I sent back some small bags of our neighbour's homegrown sweet paprika quickly made us realise that this wouldn't be a great option for us either. So we settled on no presents, on the proviso that when either Joe or myself make the rare trip back home, we would come bearing gifts. And this year gifts were brought in an abundance that exceeded the amount of clothes I brought in my luggage - bags of walnuts, dried garlands of chillies, herbs, jams and sweets, a couple of the paper mache baubles and painted 'lucky' stones for the children, all proudly home-grown and homemade.

Present buying for each other, friends and neighbours was a fairly simple hurdle to jump. Joe and I agreed that we wouldn't get each other presents in our first year, but then, feeling a little left out, we splashed out the following year and set ourselves the equivalent of a £10 budget in a superstore in town, to get some surprise treats. It's amazing how far £10 can go and be able to get the same reaction as expensive perfume or a fancy shirt. This year we went without presents again but treated ourselves to a day out in sparkly Budapest, with lunch at a restaurant and a mug or two of spicy mulled wine among the market crowds and lights at the foot of St Stephen's Basilica. Just a little something to make this wintry time feel different and special. And although it's not expected of us, we usually gift a little something to our neighbours, Tamas and

Margit, and friends in and around the village, just gift bags of homemade fudge or cookies as a small gesture of festive goodwill.

The weekend before Christmas sees a little celebration in the village square, involving small children dressed as candles, angels and Christmas trees singing Hungarian carols. Despite receiving a printed paper invitation from the polgarmester (mayor) tucked into our letterbox, we were a little nervous rocking up to the gathering crowd by the village Christmas tree, but our fears were quickly allayed with the bustle of smiling faces and rosy cheeks, some of which we knew but were frustratingly still unable to properly engage with due to our limited progress with the language. There were a few speeches and a few prayers, followed by the children's performance and then everyone descended on the treats stall. This was supervised by a handful of jolly looking women rugged up in woolly hats and gloves, liberally dishing out free hot sweet tea, mulled wine, sweets, cakes, roast chestnuts and steaming baked apples which the kids seemed to be loving. Just as we were about to sneak off home we noticed the mayor calling the children together, so we stalled for a moment, intrigued, just long enough to see him produce a large black sack and proceed to hand out toys. We were only at the square for about an hour, but as we wandered the 200 meters or so back to our warm house, weaving through excited children brandishing lurid pink cuddly unicorns and poorly assembled teddy bears, we felt a proper Ready-Brek glow of festive cheer that can sometimes get lost through overexposure to 'Christmassyness'.

December is largely about Christmas, but not solely. Little chores in the garden quite literally bring us back down to earth from our gentle revelry. Although the winter has definitely moved in, the ground has yet to permanently freeze over and we're normally safe from the serious sub-zero temperatures and deep snow until the following month. In the garden, we finish off digging over and composting any of our veg plots that still need attention and we prune back the herbs. The chrysanthemum bushes that have grown strong over the course of the year and have now finished flowering, can be dug up, divided with a spade and redistributed around other flower beds and borders and we'll reposition self-seeded fruit trees and some of the strawberry plants that are enthusiastically extending their runners beyond their allotted space. This way we're able to develop our garden with minimal expenditure on new plants and trees. We might get a light dusting of snow which will make the dull garden look stunning for a moment, until it melts, but this will act as a reminder to put the winter tyres, with their deeper tread, on the car and might be enough to push us into taking the daily dish-washing activities indoors to the kitchen table. We'll keep an eye on how the garden changes through the season, marvelling at the garlic's green shoots, planted in autumn and growing beautifully with complete disregard for the morning frosts; and the Brussels sprouts, savoy cabbage and kale that stand sturdily against the brisk breeze, providing the last of the garden's fresh nutrients. We'll begin the twice, or maybe thrice, daily activity of breaking the ice on the animal's water and if the closely monitored forecast predicts plummeting temperatures we'll take a pot of petroleum jelly out to the chicken shed and apply it to their combs to prevent them blackening with frostbite. Consequently, 'Vaselining' is now a verb in our house. We don't handle the chooks often and although they're friendly, inquisitive girls, they'll run a mile at a very fast pace if it looks like we're going to get too handsy with them, so catching them is sure to provide a good amount of entertainment and exercise. Fortunately, they don't hold a grudge though, and during the handling, we noticed that they had no more signs of any mites or lice which means they'd been clear for over a year, which also explains the swift decline in our 'sudden chicken death' problem.

With the evenings closing in and dusk arriving at

around 4 pm, we'll retreat into the house, which has retained a good amount of daytime warmth within its thick adobe walls. The bedroom, which doubles as our evening lounge, will by now be toasty from the fire roaring in the ceramic heater since mid-afternoon and the electric fairy lights make it all the cosier and inviting. Sometimes we'll play scrabble or chip away at a jigsaw puzzle with a mug of tea, sometimes we'll watch a film on the laptop and at some point, we'll put aside an evening or two to plan out the garden for the following year. This will involve a pen and paper, the list of produce that we've grown in the current year, our dog-eared and definitely-not-to-scale garden plan and any scrappy notes that we've taken over the course of the year, detailing our successes, failures and observations. We'll do a stock take of any seeds that we have left over, including those harvested from our own crops, check use-by dates and create a list of seeds that we need to buy over winter. We'll chronologize our seed packets, arranging them in order of month to be planted and we'll take a look at the garden plan and discuss positioning of the next year's crops, ensuring that they're rotated onto a different patch each year and are neighboured with companions rather than foes, to encourage growth and deter pests. I love this planning. It's a great opportunity to learn more about what we're doing and review our progress. And it's a chance to activate those grey cells which can run the risk of becoming sluggish and dust-encrusted over the often idle winter season.

We both love cooking, which is beneficial as we both also love eating, and winter gives us an excuse to linger in the kitchen for a little longer than we might in the summer months. Baking is a regular activity - other than the standard bread that we tend to bake every other day, I'll make sure that we have a tin full of ginger or oatmeal biscuits and something made with whatever we have an abundance of, maybe an apple crumble or pumpkin pie. Big vats of soups and stews make regular appearances using the stored dried beans and peas, with our dried herbs added to fluffy dumplings. Hungarian goulash is a favourite and we have most of the right ingredients stored from the garden to make batch after batch. The pantry and root cellars work fantastically to keep our paper-wrapped apples, squash, beet and sacks of potatoes fresh and although our garden produce is waning we still have plenty of bottled passata, sundried tomatoes, chutneys, jams and big jars of pickles. And every now and then we'll soak and sprout a glass jar of alfalfa or mung beans for a vitamin boost to supplement our diet.

Then there are the more rare pastimes. If I'm in a winter mood slump and need an exhilarating change, I might ask Joe to cut my hair. I haven't seen a hairdresser since moving to Hungary. Routine dying of grey hair is provided cheaply in box form from Lidl (£2 for DIY compared to perhaps £70 minimum at a hairdresser in my 'past life') and Joe has provided sensible and subtle trims several times over the years. But if I'm feeling daring, I'll hand Joe the scissors and allow him free rein. This winter Joe went about my hair styling with all the flair of Vidal Sassoon and all the skill of a slightly drunken monkey. 'Choppy' might be a good description. But it's cut, and it's hat season. The following days of entertainment and challenge provided as I see myself in the mirror and try to tame my new look is worth it at a time of the year when we all too often decide to stay inside because of the dreary, cold days. And if a haircut is not enough, there is always a little criminal activity. Since autumn we'd accumulated cuttings of trees and plants that we've wanted to propagate - geraniums and aloe vera from our own garden, plus ash and wisteria from a friend's garden. But I've also wanted Rhus hardwood cuttings, particularly after seeing how stunning the autumnal colours were, so I took it upon myself to acquire some from the village. I'm not especially proud of it, but after dark one evening I went for a wander around the block with a pair of secateurs secreted about my person. I felt so naughty and spent more time looking over my shoulder and behaving sneakily than the time it took to snip, snip, two cuttings of rose from the public border at the side of the road and snip, snip two cuttings of Rhus that were overhanging the pavement from someone's garden. No damage was done and nobody would ever know any different, except me and my hyper-guilty conscience. I scurried back home to wrap them in wet tissue ready for planting in little pots the following morning, where they sat throughout winter being analysed every week for developments.

Winter was also a great time to tackle some non-garden related projects. Buoyed by a huge success the previous year when we tiled our entire bare kitchen floor for the equivalent of about £30 using a collection of donated, mismatched tiles to produce a surprisingly smart patchwork design, we thought we would turn our attention to the 12 large framed windows that we had acquired from a friend over summer. After a long time toying with various greenhouse ideas, Joe set his sights on a small conservatory to be built against the house, partly covered by our overhanging porch. Feeling like the plan was somewhat dubious, but without any better suggestions, I accepted the windows' fate and threw myself into measuring the area up for the required timber framework and scribbling out designs on scrap paper. We bought timber from our friendly and helpful local builders yard manager, and collected a donated plastic corrugated roof from a friend who had just renovated his sheds. We had everything we needed, it was just a case of making the first move. But the first move felt like a long time coming. We measured the area again, measured our timber and spent a lot of time staring at the side of the house scratching our chins. Every time we measured anything, we seemed to get different figures. We had too much wood ... not enough wood ... the wrong type of wood. The plans changed and chin scratching was interspersed with arguments fueled by sheer frustration, which then turned into concern that our cowboyish approach would lead to a waste of money and potentially a structure that would have to be condemned from the minute it was completed. Eventually, we took the plunge. Joe constructed a frame which we then attached to the house's exterior wall and with it being suitably sturdy we then nailed on the huge single glazed window panes. The first was carelessly nailed on slightly askew, the second and third panes cracked. For good measure, we managed to fit in a squabble and a cup of tea before we got back to it and successfully attached the remaining 10 windows straight and secure. To our complete shock and joy, the plastic roof slipped perfectly under the porch overhang and rested on the frame at just the angle we needed it to be. Our stress subsided with the bulk of the structure completed and we chided ourselves for the lack of trust that we initially had in our own abilities. The next day the remaining timber was used for door frames and as slats to fill in the small gaps between lower and side window panes, leaving a grand total of no wood left over with the exception of a handful of 5cm off-cuts. I set about coating the structure with wood stain, while Joe constructed doors for each side of the tunnel-like room. Once we got started it took no more than a week to have a fully functioning conservatory area that looked smart, held the sun's warmth even on a pretty chilly day and cost just a smidge more than £100.

By this time Christmas Eve had snuck up on us and as we stood in front of the house, this time marvelling at how good our new conservatory looked and wondering how we had actually achieved it, we heard our little gate bell ringing and saw Tamas and Margit standing there with a big platter of baked goodies wrapped up beautifully with ribbon. There were the ubiquitous 'pogacs' (cheese scones), chocolate torte, assorted sponge cakes layered with cream, custard and icing, and the traditional Hungarian Christmas 'cake' called beigli, like a bready swiss-roll filled with a walnut or poppy seed filling and very tasty. It put my gift of a home crafted bauble somewhat to shame and I felt a little self-conscious as we popped over to theirs to drop it off later that day. As so often happens when we visit next door at this time of year, we came away an hour later drunk (me) and buzzing from thick strong coffee (Joe), chuckling at the promise we made to them in our first Christmas here, to be fluent in Hungarian within a year; which had been rather optimistic given our still limited, although vastly improved language skills. Regardless of the language barrier, it made us truly thankful that we had made friends with the best neighbours that we could hope for.

For the next week or so we put our feet up and overindulged in the treats posted to us from family, interspersed with some wood chopping and dog walks. We gradually drink our way through our accumulated tipples, most of which are homemade like the sloe gin, cherry-infused brandy and vodka, elderberry liqueur, rosehip syrup which we mix with sparkling water, and elderberry wine to which we add orange segments and spices while warming it through. We'll perhaps buy a bottle of unusual liqueur to try, like the very Hungarian herbal drink Unicum, or the strange sounding and medicinal tasting Wurzelpeter, pouring them over ice if we're able to produce some by leaving a shallow tray of water out overnight.

We're on our own on Christmas day, so it's a quiet and romantic affair. We'll open our few gifts, have a roast dinner with all the trimmings, call our families, message friends and watch a film or two under the twinkling fairy lights with a glass of mulled wine and a bowl of walnuts to crack. It's idyllic really. Simple and stress-free, no travelling and only ourselves to please. Of course, we do miss friends and family and the nostalgia of a UK Christmas, with both Skype and Facebook absolutely essential for us to feel connected at any time of the year, but particularly in winter and especially at Christmas. We've learnt that we can do Christmas enjoyably and cheaply and, a little like Scrooge after his ghostly visitations, we've found that the most important thing at this time of year is companionship, goodwill and making the best of what you might have available.

Babgyulyas (Hungarian Bean Goulash)

Plenty of people know very little about Hungary, but most are familiar with the delicious and hearty meat or bean stew that is goulash. If we've had a good year, we have our own carrots, potatoes, garlic, onion, peppers, dried beans and tomato passata stored in the pantry ready to throw this together whenever we fancy it, combined with our neighbour's ground sweet paprika we can create a beautifully scarlet, steaming bowl of goodness that can warm the soul on the coldest of evenings.

Ingredients:
onion
garlic
carrots
potatoes
peppers
tbsp sweet paprika
tsp caraway seeds
beans (any canned or pre-cooked)
tomato passata
vegetable stock
salt and pepper

Fry the chopped onion, garlic and caraway seeds in some vegetable oil for a few minutes. Once softened, add the rest of the chopped vegetables - I find that chunky cut works best in this dish. After a few more minutes of frying add a jar/can of tomatoes or passata to the pan, together with a cup of stock and the beans. Any beans will do - borlotti, pinto, butter beans or even a mixture are all great, but make sure that they are from a can or cooked before making this stew because they need a much longer cooking time than the other vegetables. Once all heated through add the paprika and some salt and pepper, to taste. This stew is ready when all of the vegetables are tender when tested with a knife - but if left to stand for a while, the flavours develop beautifully - it's one of those dishes that seems extra tasty reheated as leftovers the following day!

CHAPTER SEVEN

January 2016

Baby, it's cold outside

We both stood with arched backs and craned necks, marvelling between foggy breaths at how black the sky was and how twinkly the stars. The air was so piercingly cold that it stung the eyes and pricked at the nostrils enough that I had to hold back a tickly sneeze. Waves of disjointed music could be made out from the local bar on the square and there were bursts of jovial shouting as drunken locals made their way to the next party. It was New Year's Eve - the Hungarian Feast of Silvester - and we had made the decision to temporarily emerge from the snug glow of our bedroom, just as far as a few steps from the front door, to see and hear how the celebrations were going down. For a moment before midnight, the village went eerily silent, which seemed befitting for the huge night sky and freezing air. But then fireworks broke the stillness with explosions of sound and colour from several different locations, the smell of gunpowder drifted across the garden and all of the dogs of the village began a frenzy of barking in protest. We watched for a short while, feeling nostalgic about friends and family, most of whom would be celebrating midnight in an hour's time, but also wondering what the coming year would bring. It didn't take long for the chill to start taking hold though, which was when we simultaneously dropped our gaze, looked at each other and made for the warmth of the house without having to say a word.

Shortly after the alarm roused me the following morning, I sleepily wrapped myself in my fluffy robe, slipper boots, scarf and hat to venture quickly to the pantry for Penfold's breakfast and saw that the glass on the front door was coated in thick ice, both inside and out. Not only this, but the door had actually frozen stuck. Penfold shot me a look of panic and began a gentle breathy whine as I tugged at the handle, unable to let him out for his early morning wee. I wasn't sure how desperate the dog was to relieve himself, but I had images of having to give him a leg-up through an open window before things got messy. Conscious that I didn't want to shatter the thin glass, I braced one door with a knee and gave a good solid yank at the other. With a loud crack the door opened, the dog made a dash for the nearest bush and I stepped outside. The New Year's dawn was beautiful even at minus ten degrees; branches, hedgerows, and blades of grass were encrusted with icy diamonds and everything sparkled in the rising sunshine. In the pantry, I filled the dog's bowl with a generous scoop of biscuits and took stock of our winter stores. We had already moved our fresh produce into the house to save it from freezing, which this morning struck me as a sensible move - as I looked along the shelves I noticed that pickles had frozen in their vinegar, cherries had frozen in their juice and the big bottle of oil had clouded over and solidified. The dried beans, pulses, chillies and nuts seemed to have escaped harm and, ironically, the dairy kept in the terracotta 'fridge' and the potatoes stored in a big cooler-bag, had been insulated from the worst of the cold and were doing fine. Our first winter was teaching us some seriously important lessons that would save future produce from being needlessly wasted.

New Year's day was a relaxed affair involving a roast dinner followed by a long dog walk along the frozen-solid tracks at the back of the village. I stomped childishly on air-pockets in frozen puddles and Penfold skidded across them like Bambi while Joe rolled his eyes. We spotted small herds of deer leaping across the empty ploughed fields, windswept looking buzzards resting in skeletal tree branches and the usual hares and pheasants that ran, or flew, the gauntlet as Penfold flushed them out of hedgerows. It wasn't too long after we had returned home rosy cheeked and warmed our bones, that we heard the gate bell ringing and were invited next door. We were apprehensive in accepting at first, knowing our language limitations, but when we stepped into Tamas and Margit's little kitchen we saw that they had a bottle of chilled bubbly and four glasses ready for a celebration, and as the first snow of our time in Hungary began to fall outside the window, we were filled immediately with festive cheer. The room was toasty warm from the wood burning stove in the corner and it smelled of sweets, cake and coffee. We practised our Hungarian, aided by alcohol and enthusiastic mime, managing to chat animatedly about our families, the joys of British weather and plans for our garden and self-sufficient life. We had a tour of their house, met their 2 huge pigs and 5 new piglets and insisted that they come over to ours for tea the following day. It really was a joy and we spent most of the few hours together laughing which we thought was a real positive, even if it was fueled by the booze. Once the bubbly was finished (mostly by myself and Joe) and copious sweet treats consumed, Tamas thought it only right to then crack out some beer and all of his homemade tipples, including palinka and red wine. As fun as this was, it turned out the be a big mistake as we ended up disgustingly drunk in the space of two hours and after finally excusing ourselves, we wandered our way back home, stopping for a quick snowball fight on our front lawn that only briefly refreshed me from my stupor. I spent the rest of the evening either puking or comatose, with Joe, who was suffering far less, feeding me chicken soup made from the remains of the roast lunch.

The next day we didn't feel too much better and desperately regretted making plans for visitors, but we pulled ourselves together in order to get the kitchen fire going and the promised apple pie made from fruit that had been wrapped and stored successfully in the pantry since September. Sandor popped over to say hello, apparently suffering from quite a bad cold, he retreated immediately to our now cosy kitchen while Joe fetched Tamas and Margit. This took a little longer than expected as Tamas had been sleeping off a headache caused by drinking the home-made palinka that he normally doesn't touch, except on special occasions. We learned that he hadn't had a hangover for more than ten years as he tends not to drink at all, so we felt a little guilty for encouraging him. Nevertheless, our neighbours made it to our kitchen where we served them some 'English' tea with a slice of pie. We really enjoyed having a room full of people, chattering away in a language that we didn't fully understand but were no longer intimidated by.

As January progressed, decorations were taken down both in the house and the village, and the cosy cloak of Christmas quickly slipped away.

But the snow and ice was decoration enough, particularly under beautifully clear blue skies. Every morning our outer window panes were etched with an intricate lace of ice crystals and the ground kept its white blanket for the majority of our first January in Hungary. The four 200 litre water-butts set up to collect rainwater from our side and rear drainpipes all suddenly contained the largest ice-cubes imaginable, subsequently cracking the heavy duty plastic and leaking. We didn't know it at the time, but this marked the beginning of a continuous year on year winter battle of how to keep expensive water butts from breaking or buckling and if we removed them altogether, how to keep rainwater and melting snow away from the base of the house. It was quite a dilemma for us and one of the many occurrences that helped us respect the Hungarian winter. It snowed quite a few times, and only once to a depth of a foot, but it simply didn't have the opportunity to melt. Despite this though, life continued as normal in the village - old ladies cycled to the bakery, kids walked hand in hand to school in the morning, wrapped up against the elements and the village hall was chock-a-block with locals when I ventured there for my first blood donation experience. We became adept at snow shovelling after a comical start, during which both Joe and I quickly learned that metal shovels are not the best tool for the job. It probably took Tamas a good few minutes to stop himself laughing, after which he advised us to discard the spades that had accumulated so much snow that they now looked like giant white lollipops, and loaned us two wide, light plastic versions which enabled us to finish the driveway in half the time. Once we had bought some shovels that were fit for purpose, we checked every morning for fresh snowfall and were out early to clear our paths and the small section of pavement in front of our driveway, as everyone does throughout the village to provide safe non-slippy passage for pedestrians. We were always left puzzled at how, despite being out at dawn, we were always the last to clear our section of pavement. To the left and right of us the snow had been neatly piled in the gutter, with our block of snow-blanket untouched, its edges straight as a ruler. It had been done long enough ago that the ground was even dry with not a speck of icy residue to be seen. We still haven't seen or heard anyone out shovelling before us and suspect that Hungarian ice-fairies may exist. We clearly haven't been paying the appropriate taxes to secure their services.

It's hard to avoid the fact that the winter in Hungary is freezing. It's cold enough that it really must be taken seriously. But fortunately, we had done our research and prepared ourselves for the lowest temperatures and deepest snow by ensuring that we had piles of chopped firewood stacked on the porch outside the door, plenty of food in the pantry and a good range of thermal clothing, hats, scarves, boots and snow mittens. Even Penfold had a thermal fleece, that was arguably not required due to his penchant for commandeering our duvet at any given opportunity. We had nothing to complain about as we were expecting winter to be, well, like winter. We would admit to wearing our thermals indoors and sometimes hats too (although this is because we like our hats!), but both the bedroom and kitchen were very toasty once the fires were raging at full throttle. We've never had a cold night despite the thermometer hitting at least minus 15, which is largely thanks to the bulky ceramic storage heater in our bedroom; a traditional fixed feature of many Eastern European homes. Before we moved to Hungary, but after we learned of their extreme winters, I had imagined Joe and me on a rota through the night to stoke the fire so that we didn't freeze to death; but with the storage heater, there was no worry of that happening. Although it took a good hour or two to get thoroughly hot, we could stop feeding it logs in the late afternoon, confident that the high ceramic walls would still be warm to the touch the next morning. The kitchen fire was different in that it heated up quickly but consumed firewood voraciously and would lose its heat more or less as soon as the fire faded. We would get this wood burning stove going in the early hours to take the chill from the kitchen, keeping a kettle and large pan of water on it at all times, and often would cook our breakfast porridge and stews or soups for lunch to make the most of our fuel. The only room that remains a fairly unpleasant temperature throughout the winter is the bathroom; partly due to having no direct source of heating and partly due to the window being open through the day for ventilation - a necessity to prevent mould spreading across the walls from our steamy baths. I sometimes shudder at the thought of bathtime, but it's never as bad as I build it up to be. We have enough hot water to have a pleasantly deep bath and the post-soak glow lasts long enough to get dry and scamper back into the toastiness of the bedroom, where we spend the majority of our time after dark. At home, we rarely sit around in as little as a t-shirt, but if we did something would surely be wrong. It's winter after all, and its good to be schlumping around in snug boots and floppy jumpers. And actually, we both feel quite healthy and hardy throughout the season, with any signs of winter colds being shaken off remarkably quickly. It's a fairly recent phenomenon in modern society to have heaters cranked up so that summer clothes can be worn all winter long. I'm sure our forefathers would find it ridiculous, just as I'm sure that they would find my preference not to use our long drop toilet in mid-winter disappointingly weak of character.

One might assume that we dread the potential

discomfort and difficulty of winter, but for the most part, we've quickly grown to appreciate the extreme contrast from the long, warm summer months. There is a certain excitement in the challenge of making life comfortable when conditions become harsh - you have to engage with the weather and your surroundings, being properly prepared for the short window of daylight hours between dawn and dusk and not taking the temperature for granted. There comes a time when you really can't just pop out to the woodshed because even five minutes in the extreme cold can result in chilblains, so we layer up effectively and even apply vaseline to lips, nose and cheekbones when out chopping wood for kindling and certainly take extra care on our dog walks. Once we establish our daily routine of chopping wood and lighting fires we spend plenty of time inside, which is probably the hardest thing for us as outdoor types. We read, watch films, educate ourselves with online documentaries and lectures and try harder to learn more Hungarian while making continuous pots of tea. We get more adventurous in the kitchen baking different breads, cakes and biscuits and turn our hand to more time-consuming cooking, creating things like crumpets, baguettes, lasagne and pizzas from scratch. There were lots of things that we envisaged doing in this 'down-time' - painting, writing, knitting and picking up the dusty ukulele, but for whatever reason, we failed to do so in our first year. Perhaps the short days spent mostly indoors made us lethargic, but whatever the reason, we pledged to be more constructive the following year. It was certainly the most demanding time for us psychologically, spending so much time together in the close confines of the house, with so much time to think and so little opportunity to 'do'. So we were grateful when an opportunity cropped up to take part in something tradition- ally Hungarian; something that we had never even considered taking part in before.

At dusk on the Friday, swaddled in a padded coat and boots, I took my usual stroll up the gar- den path to padlock the gate for the night and glanced absent-mindedly through the naked hedgerow into the neighbour's garden. A row of three cylindrical metal wood-burners were lined up adjacent to the path; a huge, wooden trestle table was set up in front of the sheds and an old BMW was parked in the driveway signifying that Tamas's son had arrived with his family. Joe and I had been invited to help out at the weekend and this scene confirmed that we would be attending our first pig slaughter as planned, at the break of dawn the next morn- ing. Pig killings or *Disznóvágás* are a family affair in Hungary - a long-standing tradition in vil- lage gardens all around the country intended to provide everyone with sufficient meat to last through the winter. We had already over the summer heard one early morning slaughter through our bedroom walls - the unmistakable squeal followed a little time later by the sounds of a huge blow-torch and scraping - but they most commonly happen in winter when there are no flies or warmth to spoil the meat as it's processed. From what we'd seen in our village its all done in the open, where there's plenty of space and no concerns about mess. I felt a little anxious. Both Joe and I were lifelong meat eaters - we knew full well where our meat came from and weren't particularly squeamish. But we'd never been anywhere close to animal slaughter unless you include shucking scallops. Thinking about seeing a large mammal transition from alive and healthy to being dead, for my benefit, suddenly sat a little heavy on my heart and my gut churned. It would be an educational and enlightening weekend.

We had the alarm set so as to be up, dressed and able to take Penfold on a short walk before we abandoned him to our adventure. It was not yet light when we wandered next door, taking note of a bike leaning against the fence and a mobility scooter parked neatly behind it, indicating that we were not the first to arrive. It was a bitterly cold morning, remnants of crunchy snow lay patchy on the grass, perfect conditions for keeping meat fresh but also perfect for losing some extremities to frostbite. Fortunately, their wood stove was pumping heat into the kitchen and the row of braziers were fired up too, their huge vats of water already starting to bubble gently. It was 7 am, and Tamas greeted us with a big smile, introduced us to friends and family, and offered us shots of palinka as is customary before the pigs are brought out. I declined, opting for a strong coffee from Margit instead, but I noticed that at least one of Tamas's friends had been partaking of plenty of the Hungarian spirit already and hoped that he would not be leading the proceedings ... or even given a knife. Around us everything was arranged meticulously - the trestle table was covered in a plastic sheet, a range of various knives were laid out on a butcher's block, a large metal gas bottle was set up with a hose and blow-torch nozzle attached, there were plastic tanks of cold water and numerous buckets, bowls and pans. The sun was starting to rise as the men of the group began to huddle together, chat, mill around a little and then gravitate towards the pig shed. It may have been a tradition to be celebrated, but what followed was not for the faint-hearted.

The killing of the two pigs was horrific, even though it was fairly quick and no doubt a less stressful experience than for those animals who have to be transported to abattoirs for the pleasure. The pigs, one at a time, had a leash of heavy duty wire fixed around the snout and they were dragged from their pen by five grown men, which goes some way to illustrate how large these beasts were. There were loud, distressed screeches of dissent as they were hauled from their shed, but this stopped abruptly with an electric shock to the back of the neck. A knife was swiftly thrust deep into the throat and they were left on their side to bleed out while (hopefully) unconscious - the first pig within a couple of minutes, but the second took longer, presumably because the electric bolt was not as strong. It was unnerving seeing this pig continue to kick her back legs and roll her very human looking eyes for a generous 10 minutes before giving up the will to live. If you weren't viewing the scene, you may be forgiven for thinking that it sounded as if she were snoring contentedly, but seeing it first hand, we knew better.

The hulkish bodies lay on their side while, one by one, they were blow-torched until charred black all over, then scraped with knives, washed down with hot water and scrubbed to remove all hair and dirt, leaving the stiff carcasses almost white. Although at this point clearly dead, one of the pigs suffered the further indignity of having an old dry corn-cob core inserted into its bumhole to prevent leakage, while an old villager - I assume an acquaintance of Tamas and Margit, although anything is possible - wandered onto the scene, cut off a chunk of pig's ear, popped it into his mouth and began chewing on it with his toothless gums while chatting away as if the most normal thing in the world. Just when we thought that our morning could get no more surreal!

Thankfully, I could now become a little more detached and saw these bodies as meat rather than animals and so the rest of the process was really quite interesting, akin to a hands-on anatomy lesson. With the help of a wooden stretcher and several men, the pigs were hauled onto a sturdy wooden bench where Tamas made light work of dissecting the beast, with all parts being distributed into appropriate areas in an incredibly well-oiled operation. The legs were removed with an exquisitely sharp knife; then the head was chopped off neatly with a short axe and split in two across the mouth; there was a long incision down the back and both sides of skin, with its attached thick layer of fat, were removed, followed by the meaty strips of fillet each side of the spine. The carcass was then rolled belly up and all the internal gubbins were separated and removed carefully, with meat and fat tidied along the way. The only thing discarded were the intestines, trotter nails and tail, all of which were thrown onto the garden bonfire pile. The trestle table was now heaving with limbs and lumps of meat, steaming eerily in the cold air. These were swiftly prepared as joints, chops, ribs and fillets by a friend of Tamas who turned out to be very handy with a cleaver. The legs stayed whole to be salted, hung and smoked as hams in the little garden smokehouse shed. The fat was separated from the skin, chopped and thrown into huge pans to be melted down as lard. The skin would be fried as thick pork scratchings or *tepertő*. Meaty cuttings were chopped and chucked into the 'salami' and 'kolbasa' buckets, while many of the internal organs were dropped into the boiling vats of water over the braziers, to cook up for the contents of other sausages. And there was, of course, a bucket of scraps for the family dog.

Joe had assisted with much of the heavier stuff, including helping to haul the pig, scraping its skin clean and holding the carcass as it was being cut. I helped with some scrubbing of the carcass, largely as an excuse to plunge my icy hands into some hot water, but initially spent a fair bit of time standing still and watching in a combination of shock and fascination. This lead me to be colder still, with freezing toes and a numb pink nose, before being beckoned into the snuggly kitchen for a sickly sweet hot chocolate that brought me back to my senses. A little later, blood flow to extremities restored, I ventured back outside and joined in cubing up fat and trimming meat scraps for the salami bucket. This may sound like an innocuous task, but in fact it was a pretty hazardous activity with four or five adults slicing away steadily over a relatively small table. It would take just one very small careless move to find a chunk of your own forearm in the scraps bucket. The knives were dangerously sharp, the meat very slippy and my fingers freezing. In fact, I thought I had cut myself quite badly at one point, but thankfully what I believed was a flap of my own skin turned out just to be a rogue sliver of pig. I quite enjoyed my role, standing around the table with everybody chattering away, cheerfully advising me which pan each particular piece of fat should be thrown into. And in a macabre turn of events, my hands soon warmed up from handling the fat and meat that had maintained the ex-pigs' body heat. With nine adults and all the appropriate preparation and experience, it took only until midday for the two huge animals to have completely disappeared and for the area to be largely cleared of any evidence of the morning's activities, other than two bloody muddy puddles.

Once Joe and I had helped with everything that we could, Tamas continued to work outside, producing sausages from the now cooked, chopped and seasoned organs while several of us chose to retreat to the kitchen where we warmed ourselves with hot, sweet mulled wine. We were treated to lunch of some of the best cuts of meat cooked in its own fat which was very rich, but delicious and not too greasy when eaten with the obligatory bread and pickles. The morning was an amazing experience for so many reasons - the way we were welcomed and included in the event made us feel like family and we learned so much from taking part. Before the impending meat coma took hold we decided to say our goodbyes and made to leave, but not before Margit shoved a huge bag of meaty goodies into my hand. The bag contained a couple of long, thick coils of sausage, a liver and various cuts of meat and fat, which, at any other time of year we would have had to decline due to our lack of fridge and freezer, but fortunately we had some remnants of snow and a cool box. I layered the box with meat and snow, firmly closing the lid and put it in the pantry. We would be having a very porky kind of a week.

Fruit Leather

No, not for creating your own shoes and belts, but simple sweeties, similar to fruit 'roll-ups'. This is a fairly healthy treat (depending on the amount of sugar you add!) that stores well through winter and makes for a cute little gift if packaged up prettily. We had a few attempts at this before we cracked it, but the key was the drying. We found that the very top of our giant ceramic heater was the perfect spot, in winter, to balance our trays for a few days when the fruit mixture would dry out enough to be sliced, rolled up and stored in the pantry, but a long slow bake in the oven would probably work just as well and be more accessible for the average home!

You can use apple butter (see November's recipe), or any other thick fruit puree made by cooking up and blending fruit with sugar and spices added to suit your taste. We've previously made a hawthorn and rosehip version which was delicious and as an added bonus, hawthorn is good for heart health. Once you have your thick puree, line a shallow tray with grease-proof paper and spread a layer of puree across it evenly, at a thickness of about 5mm. The thicker you layer the puree, the longer it will take to dry. Place the tray in a hot dry place - airing cupboard, top of radiator/heater, or the lowest setting of the oven - and check regularly on the drying progress. The leather is ready when it's completely dry to the touch and has a shiny surface. Turn the leather out, peel off the grease-proof paper and cut into strips. Roll the strips and place in an airtight container in a cool place.

CHAPTER EIGHT

February 2017

You're kidding!

We quietly congratulated ourselves as we pushed through our second winter of snow and ice, vaselined lips and multi-layered thermals; proud that we surely, by now, would have gained the respect of our fellow villagers. We were no flimsy, fly-by-night, fair-weather ex-pats, here for balmy summers only! We were out chopping wood, walking the dog and continuously changing the animals' water bowls throughout the day as they regularly turned into huge ice-cubes that littered the whole garden and welded themselves to the ground. This year's conditions felt way more harsh than the first. We had at least a week where the thermometer dropped to a breath freezing -25 degrees. All outdoor chores took twice as long with thick gloves on; noticeably the tying of the goats' gate every morning and evening, where all dexterity was lost and both Cow and Goat would stare at us, bored and chewing, as if watching a drunk try to unlock their front door. The snow had melted and refrozen so many times that the garden paths were treacherously slippy, resulting in a spectacular triple pirouette one morning as I took scraps out to the chickens. I lay stunned, in a contorted position for what felt like forever, absorbing snowmelt and strewn with a confetti of potato peels and breadcrumbs, until Joe heard my pathetic whimperings and came to fetch me inside. There were no breakages, but I hobbled on a sore hip for a few days and for weeks nursed a large brick-shaped bruise on my left bum-cheek as it progressed through a rainbow of colours. It was a wake-up call reminding us that even the simplest of tasks could be hazardous and made us realise how much we relied on each other in these conditions. But we were nearly out the other side. With the days gradually extending we cracked on ... Spring was just coming into sight.

Our previous February had been all about the pallets. Thirty-five to be exact. Huge, solid, old wooden pallets, generously donated and delivered by the uncle of a Kiwi friend who happened to live in our county city. It was the perfect source of free, decent quality timber and went towards numerous building projects around the house and garden, including the washing up table and frame for the sink, a floor for the polytunnel, a set of vertical herb planters, nesting boxes for the rabbits and chickens, and some much needed shelves for the pantry, sturdy enough to hold the multitude of jams, chutneys, pickles and vegetables that we produced throughout the year. Joe and a newly acquired crowbar did an amazing job of carefully deconstructing the pallets without reducing the planks to splinters - no mean feat considering each seemed to be held together with a million nine inch nails and some super-adhesive magic dust. Slowly but surely, with plenty of hot tea breaks to prevent chilblaines from taking hold, new constructions took shape to make our life easier and progress our little homestead.

But this year was to be very different, there was no need and no time for building, it was all about the animals. The chickens were truly settled by this time, faring well through the cold months and starting to lay again after the winter hiatus. They were enjoying the newfound freedom allowed to them while the garden was free from crops - strutting around the crisp icy garden, taking in the air and pecking at whatever green shoots that might be available, while keeping a beady eye open should an excitable dog come lunging at them. I loved seeing them in their element, beaks down and bums up, their plumage looking like the multiple frilly underskirts of a Toulouse-Lautrec can-can dancer. Perhaps it was this extra exercise and nutrients that led to us gathering a few super-sized eggs. At almost twice the size of our normal large eggs we could have been forgiven for assuming a goose had infiltrated the flock, but it turned out that they were 'double-yokers', a real treat for us egg lovers. Less fortunate though was the fact that after a long period of no chicken sicknesses, we suddenly had a girl become very lethargic and stop eating. At first, we thought it may be related to the strain of producing giant eggs, but it seemed not, as we separated her from the others to try and coax her back to health and so as to not infect the rest of the chooks. Over a couple of days we tended to her, moving her cage into the sunshine and although she didn't get much worse, she never really showed much sign of a proper recovery either. On a lighter note, there was a haze of excitement hanging over the homestead, as we were coming into the time that the baby goats were expected to arrive. We had done our internet research and had viewed plenty of videos - a plethora of contradictory information that led us to be more confused than when we started off. We concluded, as with most experiences in our new life, we'd just see how it went. But that didn't stop us from having a 'maternity bucket' sitting by the front door from the start of the month, containing rubber gloves, Betadine, a clean dust sheet and towels. Who knew if any of these things would be useful, but it made me feel better for at least doing something in preparation.

And so to the rabbits. It turned out that the clumsy canoodling that we had seen through the autumn had indeed been that. With a gestation period of only four weeks, there was clearly a lot of practice before they eventually succeeded, but the result was a litter of seven tiny but healthy pink babies, born deep under the hay in the nesting box and well looked after by their mum. The rabbits were an absolute joy to have, partly because they were so easy to care for but also because there is not much in life more heartwarming than watching a family of bunnies peacefully crunching through their daily bundle of dandelion leaves. After we rolled up the tarpaulin frontage at dawn, they would all run to the front of the shed to sniff their hellos and excitedly wait for the ice on their water to be broken and their breakfast deposited. They were still unnamed and remained cautious of us, particularly when cleaning out their shed on a fortnightly basis, but this was a good thing to prevent them from accidentally overstepping that line from livestock to pet.

The litter had now grown into fluffy black and grey rabbits, at around ten weeks old they were more or less the size of their mum. And now it was time. After weeks of caring for them, feeding and cleaning them, giggling at their antics and keeping them safe from predators, we began what felt like the quite unnatural process of killing them for food. We always knew that the time would come, else there would be no point in keeping them in the first place, but that didn't make it any easier to do. Both Joe and I had knots in our stomachs that tightened as the date drew close that we had set for the first kill. We had discussed when, how, where and who would be killing the first rabbit and we both knew that it had to happen to call this venture a success - our own meat for the first time on the homestead. Discussing it in the warmth of the house we grew excited about having another food source. We had ideas of how to use the meat and Joe had already made the first pair of fur slippers in his head.

The day arrived for our first rabbit to be killed. After mulling over what method would be the fastest and most humane, we decided that a heavy hammer to the back of the head was the way to go. The outdoor table was prepared with a plastic tablecloth, sharp knives and various bowls. The mood that morning was serious and sullen. Joe and I had already had several arguments about nothing, purely due to the tension in the air, but we pulled ourselves together and both walked over to the rabbit shed. I pointed out a grey rabbit, as we had already established that most of the greys were female and we needed to keep at least one male for ongoing breeding. Joe took a step into the shed, slowly picked up a rabbit, took it by its hind legs and then reversed out of the shed a few steps from the doorway so as to be out of view of the rest of the animals. Feeling physically sick but with a contradictory pang of excitement, I passed Joe the hammer. Slow motion set in as Joe and I made eye contact and we nodded glumly at each other. The rabbit was calm and still, dangling upside down with its head slightly raised as expected. The hammer was lifted. Then contact - a sharp, heavy smack direct to the back of the head and the body immediately went limp. Another hit ... and another, just to be certain. Blood dripped from the rabbit's nose and a spattering was on the floor, the shed wall and the hammer. A couple of perfectly round, dry bunny droppings pattered to the floor. A macabre scene, but the hardest part was done and the tense atmosphere began to dissipate.

Once the muscle twitches had subsided, the limp body was hung by its back legs from the beam of the tool shed for skinning and gutting. The sharp knife was run around the tail, ankles and wrists just shallow enough for the skin to be eased away from the muscle and pulled off in one sock-like piece, leaving a clean, pink, naked rabbit body ready for dissecting. The still-warm rabbit coat, minus paws, was placed in one container on the table; the meaty carcass in another and the innards split between bowls for us (liver, kidneys) and the cats (everything else). The bunny paws and tails also went to the cats, who, being cats, decided it would be ideal to play with them for the best part of a week before eating them. The skin was cut and stretched out on the table and scraped as clean as possible with a sharp knife, then the fur washed in warm soapy water and hung to dry, first outside and then, when there was no further fear of dripping, in front of the bedroom fire. Strangely, I never had a problem with the butchering of the rabbit as it was easy to see it as simply meat once it was dead ... but the killing never got any easier. We were pleased that our rabbit ownership had come full circle - we had reared, killed, butchered and consumed our own animals. Being directly involved gave us a renewed respect for our animals and opened our eyes to the act of buying and eating meat. Unsurprisingly, it was with mixed feelings that I discovered a new litter of tiny black and white speckled rabbit kits tucked under the nesting boxes later that week.

It was the middle of the month when things really started to get interesting. The snow had all but melted away, it was a while since the last rabbit dispatch and just two days since sharing the rare treat of a Valentine's day meal out, so Joe and I were on good terms. I was in the process of letting the goats out of their shed and leading them to the paddock after their leisurely breakfast. There was no milking at the time and hadn't been for a few months on account of the pregnant goats needing to build their energy (and milk) for the impending births, but we were keen to maintain a sensible routine for them both. Happily, I had read up on all of the warning signs, so when I saw what could only be described as 'gloop' coming from Cow's rear, I quickly turned her around and lead her straight back into the shed leaving Goat to bleat out her lonely protests. We postponed our dog walk, lay down some fresh hay and checked on Cow regularly. It was only an hour later than we saw the first signs of hooves and a snout popping through and we were ecstatic that the kid was in the 'standard' and easiest birthing position, with front legs ready to dive out, which it did after ten minutes of pushing and loud shouting from Cow. She cleaned it up quickly and as the still-damp baby was getting ready to stand up on wobbly little legs, Cow delivered kid number two, another fairly easy birth. Both kids, soon identified as boys, were happy and healthy; walking and suckling within minutes of being born. Cow also seemed particularly content, lovingly cleaning and nuzzling her boys while emitting a sound like a low purr, like a quietly running engine. We couldn't believe our luck that our first goat birthing experience was so straightforward. We hardly intervened at all, only jumping in to give the babies a thorough rubdown with a towel to ensure that they were as dry and warm as possible in the still freezing conditions. We cleaned the shed of any mucky afterbirth and made sure that the now ravenous and exhausted Cow had plenty of food and water easily available. The kids were absolutely beautiful - we named them Bowie and Bernie and were immediately besotted. Once dry they had the fluffiest fur and the prettiest brown, black, grey and white markings. They both looked like they were wearing oversized snowboots as their hooves were too big for them. Within an hour they were walking confidently, using what looked like all their might to perform tiny jumps and starting to develop mischievous personalities. Amid the excitement, Tamas and Margit came over to see them and give some advice and noticed the sick chicken sitting in a cage in the sunshine. It was quite clear with the head shaking and the international sign of slaughter (finger run along the neck) that they thought it should be put down. And so came the downhill of the morning's rollercoaster ride! The front tarpaulin of the goat shed was rolled down for the new family to stay warm and rest, while we wrestled with how we would kill our sick chicken after witnessing such a happy and positive event.

Joe had volunteered to chop the poor thing's head off, but I found that all a little too violent. It's bizarre how I now differentiated between a 'clean' or 'gruesome' killing, but one just sat more comfortably with me. As Joe had been charged with all of the rabbit killings so far, I felt a certain duty to play my part, so I took our poorly chook out of her cage and gently stroked her head. I felt so sick being in charge of this life or

death scenario - who was I to start playing God?!
But I reassured myself that it needed to be done
- the animal was suffering and getting no better.
She was so weak that there was really no strug-
gle at all, so I took a deep breath and used all
my strength to quickly twist and pull the neck
until I was sure it was broken. I was sure. But
the bird flapped. It seemed to have more life in
it than when it was alive. Joe exclaimed that she
wasn't dead and that the head should come off
to be sure and prevent any suffering. So, with a
quick flick of an axe, the head came off. And she
flapped some more, despite without any doubt,
being decapitated. She got up and ran a bit, flap-
ping some more. It was then that we realised
that headless chickens really can run around and
that it had probably, fortunately, been dead all
along from the broken neck. To save any further
weirdness I held her body still until there were
no more twitches or flaps and she could be taken
off to be buried. We were down to six chickens.

And so the month continued. While we had the
gorgeous goat babies frolicking in one shed and
the tiny fluffy baby bunnies in another, we killed
rabbit number three. There were always nasty
arguments on 'kill' day. It was not getting easier.
If anything those little furry bunny souls ironically started eating away at us a little, so we had
to press pause and take stock. On the positive
side, it had been lovely tending to a shedful of
rabbits; they had a good life with nice food; they

were never kept in a cage; they didn't have to travel to or experience a slaughterhouse and their death was sudden and swift. All parts of the animals were used - we had three good meals from each rabbit including stews, a lasagne, a bolognese, burgers and a casserole, with liver on toast always a tasty lunch. The skins were a work in progress, with two dried and given to the dog as rawhide chews, but one fur successfully and beautifully dried and preserved as a mini-fur memento. Its been a massive learning exercise and another string to our bow - important, we think, in this self-sufficient lifestyle that we're attempting. However, there were some weighty negatives for us. Deliberately killing an animal you've reared from birth feels horrific. It's like a little piece of you dies and I had the image of the hammer hitting that animal replaying in my head for days and nights after the event. One of the main reasons for our unease perhaps is the fact that we are not starving and we don't need the meat to survive. Those stews and lasagna would have been just as tasty and nutritious without the meat. We have a pantry full of food, some of which, despite it being winter, is still our own produce; and we'll have plenty of eggs and dairy soon too. But this is the thing, isn't it? I suspect that lots of people would be vegetarian if they had to kill their own animals like back in the day, rather than buying it in nice sterile, blood and fur-free, vacuum packs. Joe and I always joked that if we couldn't deal with the killing side of rearing the rabbits, then we really had no right to be eating any meat at all. Combined with the pig killings that we'd witnessed and the abundance of other non-meat based food, we felt like we could no longer justify eating food that involved death. Meat involves an unpleasantly violent act no matter how it's done and we no longer wanted a part of it. As a project it had been a success - we had reared, bred and killed for food. We now know that we can do it if we had to and we'd learned a lot, but we simply didn't need to do it any more. Over a coffee on the evening of our last rabbit kill, Joe put it to me that we stop with the rabbits and sell them off. It didn't take much discussion. As soon as we had made the decision we felt at peace - we were now vegetarians.

We put the feelers out straight away and were not entirely surprised when Sandor keenly accepted the offer of all of our now adult male rabbits, for free, to breed with what he thought were his two remaining females, subject to checking that they were actually female. The sexing was down to me as I had done roughly 100% more research than anyone else on the matter. Sandor, with typical brute force and confidence, grabbed each rabbit by the ears, grappled them upside down on his lap, presenting me with their nether regions. I pressed a finger either side of their 'bits' to see what popped out, a little pipe or a little slit. This all sounds quite simple, but if you can imagine a large man, wrapped up like the Michelin man against the cold, wrestling rabbits the size of labradors while they screamed - yes screamed - then you have a more accurate picture. On concluding that he just had females, we agreed that he take the male rabbits off our hands so that he could continue to try breeding for himself. This left us with our two original female rabbits and the litter of 5 babies which had yet to be sexed, which didn't actually take long to sell with the help of a friend in the village. We didn't make much money, but it was better than nothing and once they were gone we were saving on rabbit feed and hay and got back the use of a shed. We still got plenty of manure from the goats, so we felt like we hadn't lost out on too much ... although I must admit it was tough for a few weeks, I really missed that shedful of fluff-bundles.

We thought that we'd already had an eventful enough month, but little did we know that we were going to face the kind of challenges that would further test our initially rose-tinted perceptions of homesteading and livestock ownership. It was just two days after Bowie and Bernie were born, Cow remained in the relative warmth of the shed with her two boys, while Goat was walked to the paddock as normal, there still being no obvious signs of her labour. So we were a little surprised on arriving home after a short visit to friends, that Goat had given birth to two babies in the small paddock shed. She had never been especially big - in fact, we sometimes wondered whether she was pregnant at all or if the movement in her belly was purely the huge amount of rumbling gas that goats tend to produce. We immediately flew into action to check on mum and babies, both girls, to help dry them out and get them into the shed together with the other new family. But we could tell that something wasn't quite right. These kids were tiny and although Goat had cleaned them up a little, they were laying on their sides and showing limited movement. More than this, Goat looked distracted, uncomfortable and on closer look, was continuing to push. We got them to the comfort of some fresh hay inside the shed where we hoped that Cow could give some encouragement, but Goat wasn't coping at all well. She had taken to laying down and was now no longer interested at all in the two babies. Bowie and Bernie had been walking and feeding in minutes, these two were doing neither and it had been hours. We thought that we'd let nature take its course and keep an eye on the situation.

Early the next day there had been no change - the kids were alive but weak and Goat was refusing to eat or drink. We decided that despite these kids essentially being the by-product of our need for dairy, we had to step in and see what we could do. It would be horrible losing the newborns, but it would be so much worse to lose Goat. We knew that we had to get some food down the babies, so whispered soothingly to Goat and then to Cow as we tried attaching the newborns to any milk-filled udder. One of the babies took some milk from Cow but we had no success with the other, and we had to be careful not to jeopardise the health of the two baby boys who were gorging themselves every couple of hours from their mum. I was starting to get particularly upset by this time, feeling helpless as we tried to use a rubber glove filled with milk as a teat. It didn't work. It being a Sunday, the shops were closed and on talking to Tamas and then Sandor, they arranged for a vet to visit but this wouldn't be until the following day. That afternoon one of the baby girls died. This was made all the more distressing by Sandor's attempt to pump milk into it's limp little body with a syringe as it was taking its final breaths. We buried her at the end of the garden with difficulty due to the frozen solid ground and stepped up attempts to feed the remaining girl, which was made easier on the Monday morning when I rushed down to the corner shop and bought a baby bottle. I regularly milked what I was able to from Goat (which was not a lot given that she was so poorly) and then stole as much as I felt I could from Cow, who was not impressed with me one bit. Every few hours I would take the tiny kid, nestle her in a blanket on my knee and hold her little face up to the bottle to help her. This was done throughout the day and then by torchlight through the evening until as late as we could manage. Because Goat was not strong enough to clean her I also did this, wiping her bum to encourage her and cleaning up with a wet cloth before setting her beside the warmth of her mum. The baby girl started to perk up, seeming stronger and stronger with each feed. The vet came to see Goat on Monday afternoon and gave various injections, not paying too much attention to my description that the poor animal was continuing to push, but agreeing to come back the next day to check on her. On his second visit the gloves went on and a closer examination done. After much manhandling he found a third baby inside Goat, which seemed to take forever to remove before being unceremoniously slung into the corner of the shed, already dead. More injections and a promise to visit again the next day. We were now not only worried about Goat, who had not eaten for three days, but about the cost of these ongoing vet visits. After the third visit and some encouragement with her favourite treat of sliced potato, Goat had started to eat and drink again with gusto, although she had no use of her back legs at all. Because of this, she was unable to feed her baby, but she was now nuzzling her and cleaning her happily. When the vet packed up to leave for the last time we were more than a little nervous, but when he asked for 5,000 HUF we were impressed. That's under £15 for three call-outs, multiple jabs and a very heavy-handed internal examination. In between vet visits we'd been bottle feeding the baby girl, hand feeding Goat, encouraging her to drink and manhandling her into different positions in different parts of the shed so that we could keep things clean. This involved getting very physical with poor Goat. I'd have to straddle her and wrap my arms around her bulk in an attempt to interlace my fingers below her belly for a good grip. There was no escape from the wee soaked fur and accumulated goo from laying unable to clean herself for days. As a result of these maneuvers I'm sure I had the smell of stale goat urine ingrained into my skin and clothes for weeks and I'm pretty sure I tore a tendon, as it was about this time that I mysteriously lost the use of several fingers in my left hand, and wouldn't have the use of them for the rest of the year.

The distress and exhaustion experienced this month could not be overstated. We lay in bed worrying about the babies and Goat in the cold shed at night. We had late nights and early mornings tending to the sick animals' needs. We felt guilty that this suffering was caused because we wanted to have a drop of milk. And yet all of this stress was juxtaposed with the absolute joy of watching the kid goats playing and the heartwarming interaction between mother and child.

The kids learned so quickly and had such big characters; Cow I'm sure looked at me in despair as the boys learned how to jump up and bounce off her sides like a trampoline and Goat, I'm convinced knew full well that we were doing everything that we could to help her and her babies. As with the killing of the rabbits, this was all part of the process. This was a hands-on education - reading a book or watching a video just doesn't do this stuff justice. We were truly invested in this process with our own animals and to experience everything first hand can ingrain some powerful messages. We got to thinking about how much suffering had happened on a small scale for our milk production and how we would have to repeat this every year. This is a continuous process after all, just like humans, goats need to have offspring to produce milk - we could only imagine the carnage involved in industrial dairy farming, where the animals are just a commodity rather than a valued member of a homestead.

By the end of the week Goat was still laying down a bit sad and exhausted, but she had lost two babies and we'd been told its quite uncommon and unhealthy for goats to have triplets, which explains why they were premature and tiny. She was eating well and looking healthier. Cow had been in the paddock each day with her now solid and boisterous boys while we were nursing Goat and we considered introducing the baby girl to the boys as soon as she seemed sturdy enough - there was such a size difference considering they were only two days older than her. With the regular feeding she quickly got stronger and by the end of the month was well out of the woods healthwise, so we decided to name her. She would be called 'Kicsiket', which means 'little ones' in Hungarian.

Winter Risotto

As you can imagine, our pantry and garden both look very different in February than a few months earlier - both are fairly bare and bleak looking, quietly waiting for spring to come around and the empty plots and jars to be filled with produce. But what we do still have in the pantry, even toward the end of winter, are several butternut squash and pumpkins and in the garden we have the last row of leeks, slightly weather battered, but still perfectly tasty. This risotto is a simple but delicious one pan dish that we throw together frequently at this time of year - proper comfort food when it's needed the most.

Ingredients:
garlic
leeks
white wine
squash
rice
bay leaf
thyme
stock
nutritional yeast
salt, pepper
(kale for an optional kale chip topping)

Using a decent sized pan (as this is a one pot dish) fry the garlic and sliced leek in a little oil for a few minutes and then throw in the diced squash, stirring to prevent sticking. Add enough rice per person and stir through for another minute or so. Because of accessibility and cost, I use white long grain rice which tends to be the cheapest option and works really well, particularly if it's not rinsed first so that the starch adds some creaminess to the dish. Pour in a splash of the wine and then a little stock, together with the herbs, continuing to stir. Allow the liquid to absorb. Now comes the gradual adding and stirring part - a little more stock, a little more stirring each time allowing the liquid to absorb and the rice and veg to cook through. This could take 30 - 40 minutes depending on your quantities, but keep going until your rice is cooked through and you have a creamy looking risotto that neither too stiff nor too wet. It's easy to adjust by adding more stock or continuing to cook for a little longer. At the end of cooking, add salt and pepper to taste and a few tablespoons of nutritional yeast flakes for a cheesy flavour. For a non-vegan option, simply stir through some grated parmesan and a little cream if you want to indulge. We've found that this risotto improves its flavour on standing for a while before serving and is surprisingly tasty cold!

Kale chips make for a quick, tasty topping for this meal. Cut out the stems of the kale and make sure that the leaves are patted dry before seasoning with a little oil, salt and pepper. Lay the leaves out thinly on a baking tray and bake on medium heat for about 20 minutes, turning a few times throughout the baking. The leaves will darken and crisp up leaving you with something similar to Chinese restaurant style crispy 'seaweed'.

CHAPTER NINE

March 2018

A little garden alchemy

It must have been a Tuesday. Meat-van day in the village. A gaggle of about seven old toothless women stood with their battered trolleys and wicker baskets at the side of the mobile butcher shop, gabbling away and brandishing empty cloth bags, ready to order up a week's worth of pork and chicken each. It was fascinating watching them do their thing as I waited in the queue, totally absorbed in what they were saying; smiling and nodding together with them. My Hungarian language was definitely coming along since the days of Tamas shouting single words at us across the fence, so I could understand a lot of what the gaggle were talking about, which was mainly nonsense gossip as I expect it would be at any meat-van around the world ... although perhaps with fewer teeth. It took so long to reach the front of the queue that I feared there would be nothing identifiable left for me to buy, but as I approached the counter there were still a few different types of sausage, so I looked up at the meat-van-man feeling like a little girl buying sweets for the first time and cleared my throat. The conversation, in *my* head anyway, went something like this:

Me - Hello!
Meat-Van-Man - Hello, bla bla bla bla bla bla blaaa bla. Hahaha.
Me - Uuuum, I'd like sausages, please. Half a kilo of these ones and half a kilo of those (pointing).
MVM - Of course, these and these, Or these? No those. OK.
Me - Thank you.
MVM - (while weighing and wrapping) Blabla blablaabla bla bla.
Me - Um, thank you.
MVM - Anything else?
Me - No. Yes. Anything else? (My plan to repeat words used at me, clearly letting me down)
MVM - So, something else?
Me - Uh, sorry, no! Thank you.
MVM - That's 1600 HUF
Me - Thank you very much. Thank you.
MVM - Thank you, blablabla bla bla bla. Hahahaha. Ha!
Me - Um. OK. Thank you. Bye bye!

I chuckled to myself remembering this encounter from the previous year as I was in another queue, this time in the post office to pay the monthly bills. We could have arranged a direct debit but had decided from the beginning that we should embrace as many face to face encounters as possible, given that we wouldn't otherwise be regularly mixing with any locals. We always tried to test our language whenever we could, whether it be the post office where I always botched up my numbers, the bakery where our standard phrase always raised a smile or the little corner grocery store, where Joe had a particularly frustrating experience one day simply asking for a pack of butter. After several failed attempts, a friendly girl behind him repeated exactly what he said and on being understood immediately poor Joe was left quite flummoxed. Our method of learning really required a decent sense of humour and a generous dollop of humility.

Anyone who knows Hungarian will tell you how difficult it is. Perhaps because it has no direct links to the Latin roots of French or Spanish that we English tend to be schooled in, or because it is so unusual, with connections to the random Estonian and Finnish but not much else. It took a year until we felt that we had a good pronunciation of the 44 letters in the alphabet, including those made up of several letters like 'sz' for s and 'dzs' for j; and the 14 vowels of various lengths and pitches. It was more like two years until we grasped some of the grammar with its flexible word order and multiple attachments meaning that words can grow to be ridiculously long depending on tense, possession and situation. The fact that you could walk into a restaurant with a cheerful 'szia' (pronounced 'see ya') and then leave with a friendly 'hallo', seemed to confirm that the language of our new home country was simply mocking us.

We watched numerous videos, flicked through books and even had a bit of a breakthrough with an online learning tool called Duolingo, on which we studied for at least half an hour every day for several years. We learned and retained a fairly good vocabulary - numbers, days and months, foods, colours, clothes, directions, and various other obscure but relevant bits and bobs. But we just had so much trouble stringing everything together, learning verb declensions correctly and understanding fully what was actually being said to us. Now, three years after buying our Hungarian house, we still could not claim to really speak the language. Certainly not properly. This may appear to be, excuse my French, a piss poor effort by most people's estimations. And ordinarily, I would agree. I have travelled a fair bit and even when only in a country for a few days I will make an effort to learn some sentences. The traveller in me would no doubt be very disappointed in these two ignoramuses, content to simply use hand gestures and smiles. But the me living in Hungary, although occasionally overcome with guilt at my lack of effort with the language, understands that actu ally, it's a little more complicated than that. We moved not primarily to be in a foreign country, but to live a different lifestyle - one which happens to involve the two of us working largely on our own in the garden. We don't really have the money to pay for tutoring which, let's be honest, is the only real way that we'd make any headway with our language skills. And we don't have regular contact with the locals that we would need to maintain a good level of practice to keep any newly acquired language skills from turning very rusty anyway. On more than one occasion I've declared a certain verb mastered, only to completely forget it by the end of the week. Perhaps its just excuses, but after a few years of coping well with the simple level of language that we had, we surrendered to the knowledge that we would never become fluent in Hungarian unless our situation changed quite dramatically.

I returned from the post office content with my social interaction for the day and opened the gate onto a garden that was just in the early stages of its magical transition from bare brown to lush green - the sad, straw coloured lawn was recovering from being frozen for months, various buds were bulging from branches and shoots were poking their way out of soggy bare earth, saturated from winter's thaw. Despite the new growth being pretty sparse and made up mostly of grass, nettles and various other weeds, seeing the assorted shades of green spreading through the garden felt good for the soul. It marked the true change of season and we were grateful that we were in the privileged position to notice the gradual changes day by day. I took in the biggest breath of sweet fresh air, puffed it out and, acknowledging that the days were definitely becoming longer, warmer and brighter, decided that it was about time to come out of hibernation. The bill receipts from the post office were quickly filed away, the budget book scribbled up to date and I stepped back into the garden to take stock of what might be done. As I squelched around the brick-lined paths and plots separated by sodden logs from our firewood pile, the most obvious job was to clear up a winter's worth of forgotten dog poo, not such a problem during the big freeze, but with garden mooching resuming and the deposits now thawed and somewhat slushy, they really had to be removed for everybody's sake. Half an hour of skilled flicking with a stick and large flower pot left the garden looking more presentable and far safer for the oncoming work. The large indoor-wintering plants (fig, lime and rosemary) were relocated back outside on the porch together with the numerous geranium cuttings, the herb garden was inspected and gently poked to check for signs of life and the door of the Tiny House (our renovated guest-shed) was wedged open for airing after a winter of harbouring various insect families. We marvelled at how the flower bulbs, garlic and onion shoots looked so healthy and were astounded that the herb garden seemed to have tiny green shoots of thyme, sage, marjoram, chives, mint and parsley ready to burst forth from their brittle stems, despite being dormant for months. I know that all of this is simply the cycle of the seasons, but the complete regeneration never ceases to amaze me. Spring for us is when the real magic happens.

Over the coming week, as the fresh sunny days continued, we occupied ourselves outdoors creating planters from spare bricks, trellis from coir rope and trying out some basketry using our bright red and yellow dogwood prunings. It was a time to do a little tidying and maintenance, fixing fences and the like, before the garden quickly turned into a beautiful vegetable jungle. Then there was the polytunnel - our homemade plastic greenhouse - created to start off seedlings when the early spring weather was still unpredictable. It had developed over the years from a simple raised bed constructed of spare bricks and homemade compost, to a raised bed covered by a large, plastic, open-ended tunnel and finally to a low-lying plastic polytunnel which was sturdier and didn't catch the wind as much, but required daily peeling back of the plastic each time we wanted to water or check on the seedlings. This was by far the most successful construction and enabled us to plant up trays of tomatoes, different cabbages, Brussels sprouts, leeks, peppers, chillies and aubergines for planting into the garden when big enough and also some celery and spring onions which would remain in situ through the summer, when the plastic would be removed completely and the area used as a simple raised bed. There was always room on the floor of the polytunnel, where we would leave pots of herb seeds and anything else that needed a helping hand to get started sprouting, alongside the baby potatoes, laid out to 'chit' or sprout, ready for planting the following month.

Winter's plot plans came in handy by the middle of the month, with the beginning of a spring-time seed sowing extravaganza. The whole salad plot was planted at the same time - several varieties of lettuce, spinach, rocket, radish and more spring onion were sown in rows marked with sticks and seed packets. Other areas of the garden had a quick tidy of weeds and were planted with several rows of green and rainbow chard, a large patch of peas and rows of carrots next to the onions already planted in late autumn, a companion planting strategy which we hoped was what kept them free of carrot fly. So far so good anyway. We do 'seed-watch' every day (despite it often being blatantly premature to do so), getting our faces up close and personal to the rows where the seeds have been planted, staring expectantly and impatiently at the mud for any signs of those primary leaves pushing through the surface. It only takes a matter of a few days for the salad patch to deliver, with radish, rocket and some lettuce appearing in neat little rows. It's at this point that I begin to feel like a proud parent and become very protective of these little seedlings, watching the weather for frosts, keeping an eye out for pests and becoming overly emotional if they come to any harm from a clumsy boot or a greedy slug. Their growth is aided by a spate of milder weather and regular gentle rain. But unfortunately, perfect weather conditions for seedlings are also perfect for the ubiquitous bindweed, which never fails to show up alongside the baby plants, regardless of our ongoing efforts to eradicate it ... and so begins the regular light weeding that will continue over the next few months.

Another reason that planting is so eagerly awaited for us is that with an unproductive garden, eventually comes an empty pantry. At this time our pantry and cupboards are at their most depleted of the year, so the planting signifies the soon-to-be replenished stocks and the need to buy less from the shops to bolster our homegrown supplies. With any surviving kale, Brussels and cabbages having been eaten and pulled up; and having made our way through the last of the slightly mottled looking pumpkins and squash, we officially have no more 'fresh' home produce available. We still have some jars of tomato passata but almost everything else in the pantry is dried - beans, peas, vacuum packed courgette, sundried tomatoes, herbs, chillies, walnuts, cherries and chamomile. We have numerous jars of pickled vegetables and various jams and apple butter for our toast, porridge and pancakes. All handy and tasty ingredients in their own right, but not enough to keep our palates interested and our tummies full. We can see a change coming in our seasonal diet from winter's root veg, squash, dried pulses and shop bought supplies, to more green leaves that can go straight from garden to plate to mouth. For self-confessed food junkies, this is an important and exciting time. But one saving grace towards the end of the month, as our first produce remains tantalisingly just out of reach, is a local delicacy that is, for a few weeks, available in abundance. It's wild garlic season. There is one particular area we know of where this pungent plant spreads rampantly and so, under the cover of a normal dog walk, we take bags and gather huge bunches of the stuff, bringing it home and keeping it fresh in glasses and jugs of water. We throw it greedily into curries and stir-fries, sprinkle it on soups and stir it through pasta as if it were green gold. But my favourite has to be a thick pesto of bright green leaves and toasted walnuts. Totally indulgent and yet totally free. In fact, it probably tastes all the more delicious knowing that it's for sale in the local supermarket for the equivalent of £1.50 a bunch.

As the warmth becomes more reliable towards the end of the month, the hammocks are strung up again between the apple trees at the back of the garden, allowing us to laze between chores and expose our ghost-like winter skin to the dappled sunshine. We're able to return to our preferred alfresco style of laundry and washing up where, surrounded by fresh air and chirping birds, it can become an enjoyable, almost meditative activity. Washing dishes at our home constructed wooden table now seems quite normal - there's no worry about splashed sudsy water on the floor and everything can be left to air dry out of sight, without cluttering the kitchen. Inside the house we have noticed the change in temperature too and soon slow to a near halt with the fire making, just sparking one up now and then on particularly fresh or rainy days.

Something that has become a regular occurrence at this time of year is the Spring clean - it's the year's first opportunity to get the rugs outside for a good beating, thoroughly dust the shelves and mop the floors with all of the windows open to air the whole house, without the risk of hypothermia. The persistent speckled black mould that accumulates on our bathroom walls throughout winter can be scrubbed away and repainted with cheap whitewash. It's one of the more unpleasant disadvantages of having steamy baths in a room constructed of mud brick, but we console ourselves with the fact that it's only for a couple of months of the year and once the walls are freshened up, its a case of out of sight, out of mind until winter rolls around again. The kitchen paintwork can also do with a touch-up, not due to mould but rather the cracking and peeling caused by the heat of the kitchen's wood-burning stove. It's all part of the package. Over the years here, simplifying our lives, we've learned to be far less precious about our home and belongings, and roll with the punches. Taking care of what we have is not a big inconvenience and neither is having a slightly shabby kitchen if we choose not to paint it one year. If we're clean and warm, healthy and well-fed, then we're happy!

As well as the superficial annual clean-up, its a good time of year for more elaborate house renovations and fixes. The frosts have subsided, the sun is often out and the heavy spring rains have yet to roll in. It was our first spring, in fact, that our house transformed from scruffy but characterful hues of pink, yellow and green paintwork to the neat and tidy cottage it remains today. I must admit that I did, and still do, have a bit of a soft spot for the Hungarian village cottages decorated in pale yellows, dusky pinks and baby blues - albeit not on the same wall - but my preference was quickly vetoed and the more understated white was chosen, with a smart and typically Hungarian footing border picked out in pale grey. We knew that we wanted the house painted at some point, but we're in no hurry. Our passion always lay in the garden work rather than house renovations, which were a necessary evil as far as we were concerned. So you can per-haps imagine how pleased we were when our neighbour Tamas - a retired painter/decorator - agreed to guide us in the right direction when it came to negotiating the trials and tribulations associated with painting the outside of a house.

We ended up making a date with Tamas to come to the local paint shop and builders yard with us early one morning, as the list of 'stuff' required seemed very long and complicated. Joe drove, with Tamas sat in the front making jokes about the steering wheel being on the wrong side and chuckling to himself between drags of his cigar-ette. Once parked up, we realised Tamas clearly knew this place like the back of his hand. He strode purposefully between sheds, calling out, pointing and poking at various sacks.

We gathered together a big bag of wet gooey white stuff, a big heavy bag of powdery white stuff, a little bag of powdery white stuff with an alarming symbol on it showing a dissolving hand, a five litre bottle of white liquid stuff, two little pots of black paint, a large bucket of white paint and a tin of dark green gloss. We had no idea why we had bought most of this, or what it was for ... left to our own devices we would have come away simply with a big bucket of white paint. But we trust Tamas, and several times he made gestures to suggest that we shouldn't worry because he'll help us. And indeed he did. We got home and Tamas told us he just had to get changed, then returned in his work gear, with several ladders, buckets and brushes - his help, it turns out, involved him actually painting our whole house single-handedly. Joe and I scraped away the top coat of flaky pink and dusty yellow paints while Tamas used a rickety wooden ladder (with questionable homemade extension) to paint the dark green fascia, after which he painted a waterproof coating over everything, mixed up and applied a plaster to the cracks and then started with the white paint once it was dry. Tamas worked on our house every day for a week. We plied him with coffee and the occasional slice of cake, but otherwise, he worked like a machine and the house soon looked beautiful. We knew then, if we didn't already, that our neighbour was an absolute legend.

It was spring two years later that the last neglected part of the house was finally getting a lick of paint and again it was neither Joe nor I holding the paint brushes. We had signed up to a fantastic scheme called Workaway, which pairs volunteer workers (normally travellers) with hosts in a mutually beneficial provision of assistance for board and lodging. We didn't have a tonne of work that needed doing, but we thought it was a great chance to mix with some like-minded people and perhaps get those tasks done that we had kept putting off. Our two Aussie Workawayers were a brilliant introduction to the experience, staying in the now cleaned up Tiny House, joining us for dog walks and meals and spending a solid few days painting the back wall of our house. No pick and mix at the builders' yard this time, just a big bucket of pre-prepared outdoor paint mix which we happily plonked down in front of the lads while we pottered off to play with roof tiles, another job that needed to be done prior to the late spring and summer deluges. Fortunately, we had learned that all that was needed in the roof was some jiggling and realignment to prevent gapping. We did learn that the hard way. After unsuccessfully using three cans of expanding foam to fill the gaps in the tiles in our first year, we happened to look out of our kitchen window one day to see a little old man popping out of the roof of his house having removed a few tiles to make a man-sized hole to work from. We felt quite foolish at not figuring out this obvious way of sorting out our roofing troubles. But, as is the case when facing new challenges, it's easy when you know how!

Wild Garlic Pasta

Much to Joe's dismay at my garlicky breath, I can't get enough of fresh wild garlic when it's in season. On a nice day, I'll often sneakily suggest an extra dog walk or cycle at a location I know is covered in the stuff, as a thinly veiled excuse to stock up. The leaves keep well in a jug or bucket of cold water for at least a week and when we really do have too much I'll make a batch of pesto - see the recipe in chapter 4, but replace the kale with wild garlic leaves. This pesto stirs into fresh homemade pasta for a beautifully rich, nutritious and fairly simple meal.

Homemade pasta is a lot easier and quicker to make than most people may think, although I'd say that a pasta machine is essential. I've tried making lasagne sheets with a rolling pin and frankly, it sucks. The key is to knead the dough well and use plenty of flour when passing through the pasta machine.

For the pasta, mix 2 cups of flour with a pinch of salt and half a cup of warm water. I use half and half wholemeal and white flour just for some extra flavour. Mix and then knead the dough well, until it feels smooth, shiny and when you pull it apart it has some stretch to it rather than just tearing. Put on a large pan of water to boil. Divide the dough into smaller balls, dust with flour and pass through the pasta machine to create thin sheets, then again through the attachment that cuts it into spaghetti or tagliatelle, draping it over whatever furniture (or a pasta drying rack!) is closest until ready to cook. When the water is boiling, carefully add the pasta as quickly as possible so that it all has the same cooking time - do a quick taste test after about three minutes, it really doesn't take long to cook at all.

Drain quickly, drizzle some oil on the cooked pasta and stir it through to prevent the pasta from sticking together. This is when you can stir in your pre-made pesto, or alternatively tear up some fresh wild garlic leaves and stir them through the pasta. Top with some toasted mixed seeds, delicious!

CHAPTER TEN

April 2017

Blooming lovely!

If there's anything in life guaranteed to put a smile on my face other than strings of twinkling fairy lights in the depths of winter, it's trees loaded with blossom in the springtime. When we're walking the sandy tracks on the outskirts of the village, glancing back over squat wine-cellar houses, the cherry trees look like fluffy clouds floating along the hedgerows. Our peach trees are laden with candyfloss pink flowers and the delicate petals of the apple and pear trees are just stretching open ever so gradually. The fruit trees hum gently - bees, wasps and other insects busying themselves with an abundance of pollen. The scattered tulips in our herb garden, remnants from the house's previous life, are bold globes of bright red and the muscari bulbs that we planted in our first autumn have multiplied along the garden paths into a beautiful purple-beaded border. The blossoms this year have coincided with Easter, so the decorated eggs, bunnies and garlands hanging in trees and windows across the village add to the colour and carnival feel. Together with the fresh dew-filled air and a lively dawn chorus of singing, twittering and cooing birds, it's almost impossible to wake up with anything other than optimism about the accumulating workload. Almost! With the heavy spring rain showers come bursts of growth in the garden that feel quite supernatural. There is a feeling of mild panic as the task list expands and we realise that the lazy days of winter when the biggest decisions were what to cook for lunch or what film to watch in the evening, are well and truly over. The lawn suddenly needs mowing after laying dormant for five months or so, all veg patches need weeding simultaneously and there are more packs of seeds waiting to be sown. We roll back the plastic on the polytunnel each morning, inspecting the seedling's growth and health, and in the planted vegetable plots we notice that the peas and potatoes are already coming up looking strong and hearty. I get anxious about seeds that were sown what seems like forever ago and show no signs of life - the carrots and parsnips - but they'll be there eventually, pushing their way through the throngs of weedlings in miniature fern-like rows. Then we can weed around them in safety, without disturbing them, and my motherly anxiety will temporarily subside. We plant rows of beetroot and corn and make sure that the appropriate patches are ready for courgette, squash and cucumber later in the month. But the burst of greenery means that this is the first month that we can start eating from the garden, which makes the work feel well worthwhile. There are young nettles growing amongst our elderberry hedgerows in abundance - wearing rubber gloves and brandishing scissors, we cut the tender young leaves and shoots and use them in potato and nettle soup, pesto and curries. Around the garden, the herbs are getting bushy and there are edible leaves that we can harvest and mix to create fresh green salads - a combination of chickweed, lambs lettuce, chives with their little caper-like purple buds, parsley, mint, dandelion flowers and wild garlic with their frilly white flowers are beautifully tasty when thrown together. It was enough to tide us over until our crops started coming through over the next month or two.

This particular spring felt all the more springy, due to our Tigger-like bouncing baby goats. Spending time in the paddock with Bernie, Bowie and Kicsiket was the best therapy you could wish for and we would regularly take half an hour out of our day to sit with them purely for the joy of being jumped on, nibbled and bleated at. The whole family was now happy and healthy after plenty of care. Goat had needed continued support making it to and from the paddock for several weeks after giving birth but ended up healthy enough to care for her baby girl and we had the pleasure of Kicsiket's company around the garden for a week or so, to give her mum some rest, but to also strengthen her little legs. She was still half the size of the two boisterous boys, but she would happily follow us around, chase after the cats and chickens and even leap around the dog. We concluded that she would very likely end up having a major identity crisis, so soon had her back in the paddock. There she would join in on the boy's fun, before getting overwhelmed and scampering to hide behind her mum, who would threaten the boys with mock headbutts to keep them at bay. As the kids grew, they quickly learned how to drink water from the buckets and eat the corn, hay and other treats given to them. This meant that they required less milk, so we restarted our regular milking practise, at dawn and dusk. The milking routine and the milk processing kept us busy. We were collecting two litres per milking - four litres a day - filtering it into plastic bottles and cooling it as quickly as we could by submerging them in buckets of cold water. After easily coping with no fridge or freezer for nearly two years, suddenly, as the temperatures rose, it became a problem and there were casualties, with lumpy or smelly milk far too regularly being poured onto the compost heap after less than twenty-four hours in the pantry. There was plenty of milk and milkshakes to drink, always a batch of yoghurt on the go and cheese had to be made at least every second day. Fortunately, I had acquired some vegetarian rennet and a packet of cheese culture for making hard cheese, which turned out similar to parmesan. These miniwheels of cheese were pressed, salted and dried for a week in the pantry, before being vacuum packed and stored in the root cellars, meaning that they would keep for a while. We also made chewy, squeaky halloumi that was great pan fried, and we accumulated jars of cubed salty feta, marinated in oil with herbs and garlic. All of these cheeses were tasty and it was a great if time-consuming, way of preserving our gallons of milk. Of course, we had looked briefly into selling it, either simply as milk or other dairy products, but there was just no demand for it in our village, and branching out to farmers markets could become expensive and therefore counter-productive on such a small scale. It only took a few weeks to realise that we had an excess of milk. Joe started to drink large glasses on a daily basis. We'd read about goat milk being lighter than cow's and therefore healthier. And everyone knows that milk is really good for you ... right?

Well as it turned out, Joe quickly developed a 'dairy belly' and subsequently became quite phlegmy, lethargic and sick. Not good. This coincided with our finding buyers for the two male

kid goats, who were becoming stocky and growing decent sized horns. We had always known
that we wouldn't be able to keep the babies.
We didn't have the space and could do without
two pungently smelling adult male goats in our
garden. We also realised that the alternative to
keeping them was their buyer most likely cooking them for Easter lunch. They were due to
be picked up in a week and we were not looking forward to it one bit. The thought of them
going broke my heart and the knowledge of their
fate unsettled my stomach - I couldn't imagine
doing this every year. I felt ashamed that it had
taken me to my middle age to see the hypoc-
risy of loving to see those beautiful spring lambs
in the fields, shaking their tails as they suckled,
and yet also loving tucking into a meal of those
very lambs' roasted legs or shoulders, with a nice
mint sauce and a glass of red. So it didn't take
much persuading on Joe's part for us to draw
a line under our goat ownership and even to
go one step further and ditch dairy altogether.
After we had sold Kicsiket as a dairy goat to a
family in the village, Sandor offered to buy the
mother goats from us, we'd just have to care for
them and continue milking until he was ready.
We slipped into a mostly vegan lifestyle very
easily from then on, eating our preserved cheese
sparingly and the occasional egg from our brood
of three remaining chickens, the rest going to
our larger flock ... of cats.

We thoroughly enjoyed our intensive but short-lived experiences in goatdom. We learned things that you just wouldn't come across unless thrown into particular situations - like how goats are great mothers; teaching, nurturing and disciplining not only their kids but others around them; and how an acute case of bloat can be eased with a good hard massage and regular strolls around the garden, burping and farting with every step (that's the goats rather than us). We both loved and hated how loud and mischievous Cow was and were grateful that she only ever escaped the paddock once, which could have been disastrous had we not been at home and had seen her as quickly as we did. I remember, one hot afternoon, walking out of the door to take the lunch plates across to the washing up area and immediately coming face to face with Cow. She looked at me, I looked at her, she chewed on some beetroot leaves calmly, as if it was her God-given right to do so, as I froze and shouted "JOE! There's a goat out, GOAT out, GOAT OUT!" She'd managed to clamber over a section of wire fencing at a point that we knew was sagging, so it was our own fault really. Both of us herded her back into the paddock and patched up the fence but remained nervous about leaving them from that point on, despite the fact that she'd only eaten a few horseradish, bean and beet leaves and a nibble of the nearest cherry tree. I always imagined if the goats escaped that they would go all Supermarket Sweep around the plots, stuffing as much as they could into their greedy mouths - but it turns out that although they can eat almost anything, they don't always eat everything - thankfully! I also learned the hard way how smart, strong, stubborn and determined goats can be at a time that I began to trust them a little too much. There was an occasion when I had gone into the paddock to give the girls a little attention - hair brushing, belly rubs and the like - and had left the gate closed but untied, confident that I was only a step away from it. The next thing I knew, Goat had opened the gate and trotted back to the shed ready for teatime ... followed swiftly by Cow, never one to miss out on anything exciting, or food related. The main problem, for me, was that I was attached to Cow, my hand clenched onto her collar in a pathetic attempt to maintain control. This wasn't a problem for her, however, as she charged through the narrow gate dragging me behind her, then underneath her, all the way to the goat shed. I managed to release and compose myself, brushing off the hay, mud and stones that I had picked up on my trip and got the girls into the shed with some bribery and mild admonishment. No real harm done, other than a slightly tender kneecap. But a good reminder not to get complacent when it comes to looking after two very smart goats.

As the month progressed, the towering acacia

and walnut trees at the garden's edge had begun to bud but remained bare of leaves. The ground was strewn with pastel petals, looking like a churchyard after a dozen weddings. With the April showers and spring breezes, the fruit blossoms had naturally taken a hit but were quickly replaced with the brightest of green young leaves and throughout the flowerbeds, marigolds started to poke their way through the soil, self-seeded from the previous year. Surrounded as we were with buds, blooms, shoots and seedlings - the beginning of the epic cycle of life in the garden - we started pondering on the birds and the bees a bit more. Well, actually just the bees. We had done lots of research into the art of beekeeping and knew that there were many different ways of producing your own honey, ranging from the most expensive and pretentious self-extracting hives to the most primitive hollowed-out logs. The more we found out, the more the whole process fascinated us - the behaviour of the worker bees, the importance of their queen, why, where and how the honey was made and also how humans had domesticated colonies of bees over the millennia. It was a Wednesday morning in the last week of April that we had our first dose of hardcore education when we met with the local 'bee man', Zoltan, the owner of a honey business in the village next to ours. A Hungarian friend had kindly arranged a meeting, which we thought would simply be a chance for us to do some costing up, but it turned out to be a full-blown Q&A session with an in-depth tour of equipment and products. Zoltan was friendly, super enthusiastic about both his bees and his honey, and as an added bonus, spoke excellent English. We spent at least an hour being shown his home-crafted hives and equipment, listening to the key processes and stages of beekeeping, taking note of tips, pitfalls and got a good idea of what our costs could range from and to. It was equally fascinating and mind-blowing. We had never thought that it would be an easy project, but we were certainly put off rushing into anything having seen the amount of effort it would take to do it properly. A bodge job regarding beekeeping felt like a bad idea. The last thing we wanted - or could afford - was to see £50 of bees swarming into a neighbour's garden the day after buying them, never to be retrieved. Over steaming tea and a few home-baked honey biscuits that evening we mulled over this potential new project and decided that it could be one for another place and another time. Although it would have been lovely seeing a busy hive in action in our garden, to provide us with a small amount of honey and help pollinate our fruit and vegetables, we didn't have a great deal of spare space, and constant human and animal traffic wouldn't be ideal for the bees or those getting in their way. We've since also found out, of course, that honey doesn't fit in with the vegan lifestyle that we had recently adopted. Maybe it just wasn't meant to bee ...

It's April when the harsh frosts are reliably over and our need to regularly tend to seeds and seedlings demands more water than our water butts hold, that we clamber into the covered manhole and turn the outdoor tap back on. Normally this is a quick and easy task, involving no more hassle than flicking away the odd fat slug that has sought refuge under the manhole cover and perhaps getting grubby knees. But we have a short and somewhat troubled history with our plumbing system. From the leaking mains pipe in our very first month at the house, to the bathroom sink's threadbare taps and a few other drips, sprays, seepages and repairs in between, there is generally at least one reason every few months for me to be sent scampering at speed to turn off the water at the mains tap on the driveway. This month, on turning on the outdoor tap, we were slightly irritated, but not completely surprised, to find that the rusty pipe leading to the tap had sprung a significant leak. I knew what to do ... so off I scampered. The manhole cover clanked loudly on being lifted, as they do, and I saw Tamas, right on cue, peer around the wall of his summer kitchen. "Problem?" he called out. "Oh, just a small problem," I answered in Hungarian. "With the tap" I added. "Drip, drip, drip" ... in English, with hand actions. Unnecessary, but to emphasise my point. Tamas smiled, removed the cigarette from his mouth and exhaled heavily. "Dripdripdrip" he repeated.

Returning to the garden, with Tamas in tow, I saw Joe had started poking and prodding around the pipe to uncover the extent of the damage. It looked as though we'd have to get digging as the damaged section of pipe extended beyond the edge of the brick-lined manhole into the earth. Reluctantly Joe started removing old bricks and mud, while Tamas contacted the trusty 'water man' - the same guy that had helped us with our very first leakage. Knowing that we were English, he brought a second cousin or some other distant relative with him, who spoke English and happened to be in the village at that time. Half an hour later, three men and Joe were peering into the hole, shaking their heads. All of the Hungarians decided that it was going to be a big problem. Maybe not a big problem, but probably a big problem. In the usual roundabout Hungarian fashion, there were several ridiculously complicated options put forward, including digging half of the garden up, replacing all metal piping with plastic and having to get a variety of various tools from various people around the county. Joe and I looked at each other in exasperation and asked why we couldn't just have the damaged section replaced. The three men nodded simultaneously and muttered, the English speaker announced "Yes, this is possible" after which they continued to talk animatedly, in Hungarian, about the more difficult, expensive and scary options. It was fortunate that we had enough experience in the country by now to know not to panic and that a 'big' problem is not always that. A small length of plastic pipe, two shiny metal connectors, an angle grinder and 5,000 forints later, we were all done and patching up the manhole and ready to turn the water back on. God alone knows what the reaction would have been to a truly worrying situation!

It wasn't long after our not-so-big water problem that we, or Joe specifically, was able to repay Tamas' assistance in an act of self-declared socialism. The little gate bell was ringing frantically, setting the dog off on an energetic barking spree that had us rushing out into the garden to check out the palaver. Without fully understanding what was happening, other than that their car was broken, Joe agreed to help and found himself providing a driving service for the best part of the morning. He took them to the nearest big town to go shopping, picked up their daughter from the train station and collected a car battery from the garage (which explained the need for the favour). It's with a happy heart that we offer and provide assistance as they've always been so good to us, but they did seem incredibly grateful. When he got back home, Joe was offered a huge hunk of their finest home smoked, home reared ham ... but it was turned

down with some scrappy but polite explanations ... else we'd be very undisciplined vegans
indeed!

Warm Herb Bulgar Wheat Salad With Toasted Seeds

The sun is out, there's loads to do in the garden and the herbs are getting bushier by the week. On a busy day, when lunch creeps up on us and we want to throw something quick, tasty and nutritious together using what we have available from the garden, this is one of our satisfying go-to fixes.

Ingredients:

bulgar wheat
lemon juice
olive oil
a generous bunch of parsley, mint and chives
sundried tomatoes
toasted mixed seeds - sesame, flax, sunflower and pumpkin work well

Cook the bulgar wheat according to the pack instructions, then drain, it should take no longer than 10 minutes. While the bulgar is cooking, toast the mixed seeds a frying pan without oil until they brown slightly - you might need to stir and toss them so as to toast them evenly and prevent them popping like popcorn. Wash and chop the herbs and slice the tomato, then mix these into the cooked bulgar wheat. At this point, you can add other vegetables like olives, grated carrot, sliced celery. Drizzle some lemon juice and olive oil over the salad and then shake the toasted seeds over the top.

CHAPTER ELEVEN

May 2016

From the rat race to a snail's pace

Nearly a year after moving to our little Hungarian homestead, it wasn't uncommon to lose track of what day of the week it was. I should clarify that this was because it wasn't especially relevant to us, rather than being early onset Alzheimers. It became less important to keep track of time because we seemed to suddenly have such an abundance of it. We were loving our change in lifestyle and missing very little. We felt better - healthier and stronger, with clearer skin, toned muscles, wider smiles and a bouncier dog. But there was something that felt quite new to us as the year milestone approached. The anxiety around not receiving a monthly paycheck was starting to ebb away. Curiously, the more distant my old working life became, the less we were worrying about money. This was no holiday anymore, the safeguard of my twelve-month sabbatical was nearly over but I had absolutely no intention of returning to my old office desk in London. Perhaps we were enjoying ourselves too much ... or maybe we were starting to make this lifestyle work and we could see this as being our future. Either way, we were getting a handle on our financial fears - the first few months were expensive as expected, but once the house was decorated and we had settled into a bit of a routine we were seeing our costs reduce dramatically. We kept a budget book, in which we wrote every single payment, from a tank of petrol to a crusty loaf from the local bakery. Our monthly bills were just for electric, water and internet; with annual bills for car insurance and the Hungarian equivalent of council tax. Even with more crops in the garden we still had to buy some groceries each week, plus animal feed. And now and then we would have significant purchases, like a bulk load of wood, or the electric lawnmower. But overall we knew our costs were lower than they ever were in the UK - mainly because we have no rent or mortgage payments. Our outgoings over the first (nearly) full year averaged at around £640 per month, but excluding those first few months, it was nearer the £400 mark. As time went on, we produced more from the garden, cut costs by cycling wherever possible rather than taking the car and were more conscious when grocery shopping - focusing on local, seasonal and reduced products, always selecting the cheapest options. We set ourselves an ongoing monthly budget target of £200. Often we would overspend by a little, but sometimes we spent even less. Whilst neither of us had an income we were acutely aware of the bank account emptying slowly and knew that we would never be self-sufficient enough to prevent this from happening. Paid work would have to be factored in at some point. But we also knew that point could be a long, long way off. The house we had sold in the UK, even with a hefty penalty for withdrawing from the mortgage early and the exorbitant estate agent fees, had made us enough money to sustain this lifestyle for many years yet. Perhaps even until we were satisfied with it and ready for the next challenge!

All this talk of money, you'd assume it was the most important thing in the world. I feel it's a shame that polite society has developed in a way that this isn't far from the truth. Eventually, in our new life in Hungary, Joe and I realised that our time is worth so much more to us than any money we could either earn or spend. We had made the immediate trade-off of more time for less money, but with the massive bonus of being able to spend both on what we wanted to. We would have the same 24 hours in a day that everyone else in the world had, but we had actively chosen to use it differently. It changed everything...

I wake naturally at dawn, about 5 am in late spring, before the sunrise but at a time when there is a soft light penetrating the drawn curtains of the bedroom. There are no aggressive alarms shocking me from my dreams and perhaps thats why I don't feel any reluctance or resentment as I reach for my dressing gown and wander drowsily to the front door. I slip my bare feet into boots or flip-flops, whichever are closer, and I gather tubs and dishes of animal feed from the pantry and grab the full watering-can, sat under the outdoor tap. The cats and dog have their bowls of biscuits, the chickens are given their grain and the rabbits have the front tarpaulin of their shed rolled up and a few cobs of dry corn thrown in for them to nibble. All water bowls are refreshed and I wander a little less drowsily now back to the house, taking a quiet moment to appreciate the fiery orange glow of the sunrise creeping over the garden gate and smile at the fact that though it might be early, I rarely, if ever, have to get up in the dark anymore. Inside the house, a pot of tea is made and two cups are brought back to bed to drink while we catch up on news and messages. There's no urgency to get up and out as we're working to our own schedule rather than anyone else's - we know what needs to be done for the day, and have the whole day to do it.

After a leisurely cup of tea or two, I get out of

bed again and dress for the day, but there are no fancy corporate work clothes now. I don't have to colour-coordinate, make myself presentable with make-up or cover myself with deodorant and perfume. Bad hair days can be hidden under a cap. I don't need to keep a constant stock of ladder-free tights or have piles of washing accumulating from wearing a new blouse every single day. I might take a risk and wear that t-shirt with a bit of a tea stain on it and the jeans with a muddy paw print - I'm working in the garden after all. If I'm feeling particularly carefree I'll go braless ... that's something I couldn't do in the office. Well, not without serious repercussions anyway. This new routine is far quicker and my wardrobe is way cheaper to maintain, not to mention so much more comfortable.

The hour commute into London from my Essex home wasn't excruciating on a good day. I'd usually get a seat and be able to snooze or read the paper on the way and being wedged in the hustle and bustle made me feel part of something vaguely interesting and important, even if in reality it wasn't. But delays and cancellations were more frequent than they should have been, the annual ticket cost me 10% of my salary and there were plenty of things I'd rather be doing. I've swapped my commute for a country dog walk. An hours stroll can take us around the fields of sunflowers and corn, get the blood pumping and leave the dog flat out for the rest of the day. I guess my new commute is stepping across the porch and into the garden with a steaming cup of coffee in my hand ... far preferable to accidentally falling asleep and dribbling on the shoulder of a stranger on the 06.56 from Chelmsford.

My 'office meetings' are arguably more productive now than ever before, just Joe and I mulling over the day's to-do list while eating porridge with jam for breakfast. There are never any unnecessary meetings, nobody is absent, late or unprepared and we tend not to have any meetings that are solely for setting out further meetings later in the week. My regular breaks throughout the day are similar in that I do still drink a lot of tea and coffee, but instead of sat in front of the computer battling with excel spreadsheets and deleting emails, I'm leaning against my garden fork, watching flocks of as-yet-unidentified birds fly overhead in a perfectly co-ordinated 'V' formation. More often than not my London lunch would be taken at my desk, either last night's leftovers, an uninspired sandwich from home or an extremely overpriced one from the nearest Pret. My Hungarian lunches are proper meals - home grown, home cooked and eaten unhurriedly at the kitchen table. We have that time to cook good food and bake tasty treats - so much healthier and cheaper than buying everything pre-made. I don't miss those accumulated expenses of office life - the quick but numerous coffees out; the birthday collections for people you hardly know; the kind-of-obligatory voluntary contributions to charity runs, leaving or maternity gifts or morning teas that seem to come around all too frequently. Life was so expensive. I earned a good wage but felt cheated that I was regularly left with not much to show for my long days and so much being spent on things I didn't really want.

In the UK, we were required to cram our real lives into evenings, weekends and holidays. Household chores and maintenance, social and leisure activities, keeping in touch with friends and family, exercise, hobbies and interests - those things that you really wanted to be doing - forced into nuggets of time at the end of the day or end of the week when actually all you needed was some rest. We were in the habit of booking holidays and weekend breaks to get away, to recharge from the life-sapping job. I understand holidays to explore and travel, but to escape? To actually escape everyday life in order to relax? Wow. Surely we're doing something wrong if an escape is needed on a regular basis - something to look forward to in order to keep you going. Of course, it wasn't exactly a hellish routine and most of the time I was genuinely happy, but all too often there was a feeling of .... well, I suppose it was adequacy. It was just a little unsatisfying, unchallenging, easy. We needed a wholesale change. Not just to acquire an allotment and go part-time, but a proper, smack-in-the-face, scare-the-crap-out-of-you change.

So here we are, nearly a year after giving up the rat race. Things are done at our own pace. We work hard sometimes, but it never feels like work because being outdoors and learning to be more self-sufficient is something that we both love. Our work is varied, educational, challenging, continuously changing and we have the freedom to be creative as the urge takes us. We've learned to love daily menial tasks and find contentment in the simplest of things. Having no regrets is putting it mildly, this really feels like how life should be. And we still haven't scratched the surface of all the exciting potential that this way of life may bring. There have been sacrifices - we certainly don't spend much money and we don't venture out often, but we don't feel like we go without anything that we need, or really want. We've just stopped wanting so much, which is incredibly liberating. It turns out I love living barefoot and pooing outdoors. It has a primaeval feel about it. Back to basics.

Everything feels very normal for us now. The only time we're reminded that we do things slightly differently is when we have the pleasure of friends and family coming to stay with us. The initial tour has to include explanations of how and when to use the outside long-drop loo,

why we're a strictly 'no double dipping' household and how sparing we have to be with the
hot water. It feels a little ridiculous at first, but
it's actually fantastic for bringing people down
to earth. There's no room for snobbery and it
quickly instigates an appreciation for the simple things - like food, shelter, warmth, being
clean and feeling loved. And it's not like we're
living in a cave and cooking over embers, or we
wouldn't have super-speed internet!

There's something in particular that we're able
to do that aligns with our self-sufficiency and
cheap living that we especially love, and that is
cutting out the middleman. Instead of working
a job to make money to buy our food, we simply produce it ourselves. This has worked bril-
liantly on a larger scale too, when we've helped
out our friends and neighbours. Whether it's
planting an acre of paprika with Tamas in spring
or digging and bagging up his potatoes in late
summer; or picking cherries, sunflower heads,
and corn in Sandor's fields at various times of
year, we are guaranteed to be rewarded with a
sack of produce that seems to far outweigh the
couple of hours work taken out of our day. Naturally, we'd do it gladly for nothing. It's always
a pleasure to be working outside in the sprawling fields, a totally different environment to our
little garden, feeling like we're making a contri-
bution to something. But it does also feel like
sticking two fingers up to The Man having our

pantry full of goodies without having to pay a forint for them. In later years, the vegan thing would come to completely baffle Tamas and Margit of course, being unable to offer us hunks of meat for our occasional assistance, but this hasn't stopped them from going home and returning with bags of frozen vegetables and on one occasion a bottle of fizzy wine to share with some Workawayers who had also lent a hand. When we're in Sandor's fields with him, he seems to like practising his English on us and sharing his worldly philosophies, one of which is that we should be looking for paid work. "Everyone must have a job" he grumbles, showing his frustration at our frivolous unemployment. But we didn't need jobs, either for the structure, the challenge, or the money. We have enough. And as it turns out, enough *is* enough.

*****

May is most often hot. Temperature-wise, it's the month that starts to really mark the difference between the average summer in the UK and that in Hungary, where the thermometer regularly creeps up to the high twenties, only to be broken every so often with one of those epic downpours that turn the storm drains into whitewater rapids. It's this perfect combination of warm sun and intermittent drenching that throws the garden into overdrive and makes it probably our busiest month. More or less everything is planted up by the end of the month - the squash, courgettes, dry bean varieties and dwarf beans are sown and the little brassica seedlings are pricked out and planted in their respective patches, as are the leeks, tomatoes, paprika and aubergine. We start to harvest the salad crops now that the radish are plump and the lettuce, spinach and rocket are ready. The herbs that are getting beyond bushy are chopped back for the first of many times, tied into little bundles and hung under the porch to dry in preparation for the winter months. Delicate sprays of cream-coloured elderflowers start to bloom amongst the hedgerows, giving off a heady, sweet perfume that just begs to be made into cordial and sparkling wine. Being our first May in Hungary, we were still making new exciting discoveries in our garden - it turns out that the unidentified tangle of brambles at the edge of the garden was actually a raspberry patch, with fruit taking shape but not quite ripe enough to pick; and that delicate, frilly plant that I poked and prodded, trying to identify the previous summer was actually a giant asparagus that had gone to seed. Our asparagus patch didn't actually amount to much, with one little phallic protrusion pushing through the soil at a time, but they sure were tasty. Sometimes they would be lucky enough to be sliced up and sprinkled on some salad or pasta, but more often than not they wouldn't get as far as the kitchen. Whoever got to the stem first would slice it off at the base, snap it in two and together we'd shove it into our mouths and enjoy the green crunchy sweetness al fresco. Our little homestead plot really was the garden that kept on giving that first year, but the highlight probably had to be the fruit that was already established ... and in May that meant foraging through a huge jungly strawberry patch. We had low expectations given that we didn't know how long the patch had been there, nor how productive it may have been in the past, but we had noticed plenty of flowers the previous month and had our fingers crossed. By the end of that first May, we had jars of strawberry jam filling the pantry in addition to having fresh berries on our muesli every morning for weeks and a bowlful temptingly placed on the table to pick at throughout the day. Such a treat!

Together with all of these garden goodies though came the seemingly never-ending cycle of weeding, lawn mowing and watering - a routine that continued through until the end of summer. Sometimes it felt like an extended Groundhog Day - more a Groundhog Week. By the time all of the plots were weeded, the three sections of lawn mowed and the paths and borders trimmed we had to start all over again to keep the garden tidy and ensure that the seedlings had the best chance of growing. It was hardly a burden though, out in the sunshine, working our way down rows of plants, feeling in touch with nature Watering was a pleasure too, once we got used to how long it took us using watering cans rather than a hose. It was a deliberate decision sticking with the more manual approach - our garden was tricky to get around anyway, but walking up and down the rows to water means you know exactly where the water is going (so the veg gets watered rather than the weeds) and we can keep a close eye on how everything is doing. We watered first thing in the morning, my favourite time of day when everything is cool, quiet, dewy and smells fresh and the plants, in theory, get the most benefit from the water. The added bonus was that we'd gain nice toned arms from repeatedly hooking the water from the water butts and carrying the cans around the garden.

We had a good collection of water-butts in our first year to supply our regular watering - giant, green 200-litre capacity plastic buckets placed under our two drainpipes. One was squeezed underneath the end of the pipe that led from the front-facing roof, with a piece of hosepipe to direct any overflow away from the base of the house. Another three were lined up at the back of the house for the rear-roof's rainfall - one directly under the drainpipe and the others connected by short strips of hose-pipe that would take the overflow from the neighbouring tanks - these never had an opportunity to overflow; the heatwave that first summer made sure of that.

Our biggest problem was that the water collected after a short but intensive storm could, within days, turn into a murky, stagnant, stinking soup ... fine for the garden, but not a treat for the senses, nor was it great for the other jobs we often used fresh rainwater for, like our weekly laundry. If we absent-mindedly chose to rinse our hands in the water-butt after a morning of weeding, we'd often be rewarded with a lingering stench that could not be washed off without several rounds of scrubbing with soap and a nail-brush. Water from our outdoor tap was connected to the mains and it was this that we used when our water-butts were down to their final dregs. Despite knowing at the time we bought the house that we didn't have a well or water pump in the garden, it was still a disappointment to us, knowing that so many other houses had them. We looked into having one drilled, but it would be a costly and messy exercise, made more difficult than usual due to the house being on a slight hill and therefore further from the natural water table. Water wasn't expensive, but it would have been an added bonus for us to be able to further reduce our costs and use untreated water on the garden. But as it was, at least after a good storm we had around 800 litres of water to use. Little did we know at this time the future hassles that we would have with these water-butts each winter, with even the slightest rainwater in them expanding as it froze and breaking the plastic, leaving us with a recurring and eventually expensive crack habit.

It was the first May at our homestead, as we were settling into these leisurely garden routines, that we unwittingly acquired the first of our many cats; and as with most of our experiences in Hungary, it didn't happen in the most straightforward of ways. It was early evening and we were about to sit down to eat when Penfold decided to bark incessantly at the gate, to the point that we could no longer ignore him and went to investigate. What his long lurcher nose had sniffed out, were two tiny, quivering kittens curled up together on our driveway beside next-door's fence. They seemed to be no more than a couple of weeks old - their eyes still closed and their meows no more than feeble squeaks. We left them for a short while, hoping that their mum may have been in the process of moving them, but as dusk crept in, it didn't feel right to just leave them there. We scooped up the little scruffbags and placed them on an old towel in a cardboard box and brought them inside, while we went back to our meal and a fresh discussion on what to do with our find. What was clear, despite my brother's sarcastic warnings about how we may end up inadvertently becoming a retired donkey sanctuary if we started to take in all the village's waifs and strays, was that we had to at least nurse the kittens to health. Cats are not high on the agenda for care in rural Hungary, treated more like vermin than pets for the most part. You would be hard pressed to pay someone to take even the cutest fluffiest kitten off your hands and organisations like the RSPCA are few and far between, certainly beyond the cities. We both love cats, but they were never part of our homestead plan and we worried that Penfold would be continuously chasing them. We didn't want them ravaging our lively little ecosystem or leaving their poorly covered poo littered around the vegetable plots. This turn of events was really quite a nuisance for us ... but being the softies that we are, we soon settled into what would become several weeks of intensive kitten surrogacy. There were never-ending mornings of wiping their closed pus-filled eyelids with salt water solution, coaxing the pair to suck milk from cotton buds until we created a little pipette for the purpose, wiping their bums to encourage them to poo and pee and give them some love and attention throughout the day. We named one Winston and one Fergusson and became way too attached to them. This became clear very quickly when we realised Fergusson wouldn't make it, as he just refused to eat or drink and became weaker and weaker until he didn't wake up one morning. We dug him a little kitten sized grave and buried him with a few chive flowers, sad that we had failed him and that Winston was now on his own. But he wasn't on his own for long, for one single day after Fergusson died, his doppel-ganger dropped from next-door's roof and began yowling outside our gate. Joe and I both witnessed this strange turn of events and decided that we wouldn't, this time, get involved. At which this new kitten scuttled under the gate and straight to our feet. And so Fergusson II joined the family and the bizarre routine continued. The pair progressed onto canned cat-food after a couple of weeks and seemed healthy, albeit with some residual gluey eye problems, which led to a hilarious morning routine. I would open their cage and on my call of 'kittens' they would dash at an excitable speed towards my voice and their waiting bowl of jellied meat, sometimes veering off course and hitting various obstacles en route like little fluffy bumper cars. Once at their food they would basically lay in it, chomping frantically until it was gone and they were left caked in gravy, their bellies plump, ready to be wiped down with a wet cloth ... although Penfold did try to volunteer for this task. Fortunately they grew strong fairly quickly; their eyes opened and gradually cleared of any stickiness and they were big enough to venture outside during the warm, sunny daytimes. We monitored them fairly closely when they were outside, letting them climb, play and learn but it was so difficult not to intervene when they decided to clamber to the very top of the pear tree, wobbling and mewing triumphantly as I covered my face with my hands and peered nervously through my fingers. Their education came thick and fast when each of them was treated to an impromptu trip up the garden between Penfold's teeth, as their squeaks, mews and shenanigans became just too much for him to ignore. They were fine though, and for the most part Penfold looked out for them, even allowing them to curl up with him on his sheepskin rug on occasion. Soon they became the 'outdoor cats' that we intended - happily sleeping and eating outside, gallivanting in the garden at dawn and dusk, draping themselves around each other and the porch during the hot days, making themselves available for cuddles whenever possible. Winston would sit on on my discarded flip flops and watch me as I weeded the garden and Fergusson had a habit of jumping onto my back and getting curled up comfortable in the crook of my neck, no matter what job I was trying to do. And so they became an integral part of the garden. Even though we never wanted cats and could certainly have done without the extra mouths to feed, they've been great ratters and 'molers', surprising companions to Penfold and their crazy personalities became irresistible. We've since found out ... the hard way ... that both Winston and Fergusson II were female. But now it wouldn't feel quite right having a homestead without at least one feline slinking around the shadows and my call of 'kittens!' is still guaranteed to have at least one happy cat leaping from the undergrowth for some love.

Elderflower Fizz

The first batch of sparkling elderflower wine we made had us hooked immediately - we've made it every year since. It's light and sweet, perfumed and refreshing, only mildly alcoholic and is just the perfect drink to sip on a late spring evening. A word of caution though, particularly if you, like us, don't have a fridge. Our first ever batch was made during a particularly warm May and when ready, was siphoned off into various types of glass bottles, some of which had clip tops. What we didn't know then, was that we had created several elderflower bombs that sat in our pantry, and after a few weeks of warmth, exploded in a sticky and lethal mess of glass and syrup. Fortunately we heard the incident from the safety of our kitchen, but whenever we've made further batches we make sure to let out some of the pressure before it gets to explosive levels. My simplest advice though ... if you have one, keep it in the fridge!

ingredients:
8 blooming elderflower heads
800g sugar
3 or 4 lemons
water

Dissolve the sugar in 2 litres of warm water, then top up with a further 3 litres of cold water. When cool, add the zest and juice of the lemons together with the flowers and stir. Leave this mixture for up to a week - some activity (fizzing/frothing) should happen after a couple of days, but if it doesn't this is when you can add some champagne yeast to help the brew along. We've never had to use any, with the natural yeasts on the flowers proving sufficient enough to ferment the brew. After a week, strain everything through a clean muslin cloth and bottle the liquid in clean glass or plastic bottles with secure lids. It's ready to drink after a week and can keep for many months if stored in a cool place. I think that it's a drink best enjoyed young, rather than being a keeper to store to a vintage age ... if it doesn't explode before then anyway!

CHAPTER TWELVE

June 2017

Making hay while the sun shines

My bare feet were planted firmly on the dash-board and with the window wound down low the wind was lashing at my hair, whipping it into messy knots around my sunglasses. I rested my head back and stared up at the endless blue of the sky as the walls of tall green corn either side of the car whizzed past. Cresting a gentle hill and heading north-west away from our village, we have a perfect view over hectares of sunflowers, their huge golden faces shining upwards in unison, creating a glorious yellow blanket across the fields. Onwards we passed slowly over train tracks, through a small town and a couple of villages before reaching the outskirts of Lake Balaton. After a couple of turns and some winding tree-lined roads, we come to the south-eastern corner of the lake, where we turn off and drive down a long sloping road towards the water - it takes about half an hour to get here from home. On a hot afternoon in a car with no air-conditioning, it's not a pleasant drive, but we've decided on a morning visit today. Dawn in June arrives rudely early, creeping in through the bedroom windows at 4.30. But waking with the sun is such an organic process that we're happy to get up and tend to the animals in the pink glow of the sunrise. After some coffee and toast, we can comfortably complete several garden tasks, take the dog for a walk and still leave the house before 9 for a morning at the lake. And so here we are, parking up on a dusty patch of ground under some shade, excited to have a rare break from the garden for a swim and relax. There are few free places to swim at the lake, despite its 235-odd kilometres of shoreline. The waterfront tends to be taken up by large expensive properties (which mostly stand empty for six months of the year), long stretches of tall, wild reedbeds or pay-to-enter beaches, like this one. It doesn't look like we're at a beach, in fact, the towering grey concrete slab of a building that houses the tiny ticket booth and changing rooms is pretty intimidating, looking like a harsh throwback from the communist era. If we didn't know better we'd stay well away! But after we walk up the concrete steps, pay our fee and walk down to access the lake on the other side of the building, an oasis opens up. The grass is lush and well kept, spreading right up to the front of the lake. There are willow-like trees providing dappled shade in rows all along the waterfront. There are playgrounds and sandpits for the kids, loungers for rent, a small selection of cafes and bars offering coffee, beer, chips, hamburgers and the ubiquitous langos - deep-fried dough slathered in garlic oil, sour cream and grated cheese - a Hungarian delicacy guaranteed to provide enough calories to keep you swimming all day, or floating at least. A bored-looking lifeguard sits at his station under a tree tapping at his phone, but otherwise, at this early hour, there is hardly anyone else here. It's a marked difference compared to how crowded it can get in the real heat of the day when the water is a colourful frenzy of laughing, splashing and inflatable unicorns. Right now it is so peaceful, the lake surface is glassy and unbroken, so inviting. There are numerous thermal hot springs and spas around Hungary and to relax in steamy water under starry skies or a flurry of snow at Budapest's Szechenyi baths in winter is pretty special; but I'm not sure that there's anything to match the perfection of a simple swim in an empty Lake Balaton on a hot summer's morning. There's no sand getting in places it doesn't belong, no chemicals or sticky saltwater residue and the lush greenery of the shore counterbalances the glare of the sun and creates a soothing Eden in which to chill. We'll have a leisurely swim and float about in the cool shallow water before drying off in the sun, perhaps repeating once or twice more before grabbing a cob of hot juicy sweetcorn from a nearby vendor and heading back home feeling refreshed and satisfied for the rest of the day. Even on our tight budget, we think the 400 forint entrance fee is well worth the money on the odd occasion, we don't aspire to be complete hermits after all!

It feels a particular treat to escape to the lake now - having had the goats to look after for the past nine months, we felt it ill-advised to go anywhere for too long - an hour shopping trip or dog walk was about the limit of our comfort zone when it came to trusting them, particularly after Cow's recent escape. But now they're gone, since Sandor finally arranged some housing for our two remaining mama goats on the expanse of land behind his house. It was only a week ago that we took them on the slow trot from their pen to Sandor's, leaving perfectly round pebbles of dry goat poo along the pavement that would remind us of them over the following few days. The garden has been eerily silent without the girls and there's a slightly melancholy air over the place, albeit tinged with relief that this episode is over. A little like when all the family go home after a long Christmas visit, leaving the house suddenly empty and quiet. But at least we know that they'll be well looked after and there's always something to do to keep us occupied ... and in June, its kilos of cherries.

Hungary is covered in cherry trees, which goes some way to explain why the Hungarian countryside can be so picturesque in spring - the blossoms seem to border every road in every village and gardens through the country are sure to have at least one cherry tree, of either the sweet *csereszne* or sour *meggy* variety. We've learned already, after just a couple of years, that stone fruit can be a little hit and miss - last spring some of the blossoms in our garden were turned brown overnight by an unexpected late frost and those flowers that did survive and developed into tiny baby fruit-buds then took a battering during a week of high winds, leaving them strewn under the trees. We must have harvested a single cup of fruit from each cherry tree and had not a single apricot, peach or plum. But there is little you can do against the forces of nature, other than be grateful when a good crop comes along. Like this year.

We'd already picked several jar-fulls of sour cherries from the five trees in our garden - a modest amount really, but enough to have some to enjoy fresh and some to cook into a deliciously spiced cherry soup while preserving the majority by bottling. But the real challenge in cherry processing came when Sandor asked if we would like to attend to the tree at his little vineyard plot located on the dusty trails on the outskirts of the village, as he had neither the time nor the inclination. We gleefully accepted, happy at the prospect of a bag or two of free fruit. Not just fruit, but beautiful, glossy, plump crimson cherries. I love cherries, but they've so often been way out of my price range, even when I've been working, so this sudden excess felt like quite a blessing. Early the following morning we loaded the car with buckets, ladders, a few bottles of water and an excitable dog. It took just 10 minutes to drive around to Sandor's plot, we could have got there faster, but decided the risk of filling the car with dust and sand from the road wasn't worth it. We parked up and took in the idyllic view across the village's collective vineyards - there were certainly worse places to be of a morning. The sun was already warm and drying off the dew on the grass and vine leaves as we set up our ladders beneath the huge cherry tree. There was just one tree, but she was a beauty - old, gnarled and laden with fruit. Penfold was released and bounced off, disappearing into the surrounding fields of corn, while Joe wasted no time in climbing into the depths of the tree's branches with a bucket, soon completely hidden amongst the foliage. Not a fan of heights, I skirted around the base of the tree, picking fruit that was at arms reach, or available at just a rung or two up the step-ladder. We worked swiftly, hypnotised by the repetitive plucking of fruit, enjoying the surrounding birdsong, crickets and cicadas, the fresh air, the sun on our skin and the numerous rogue cherries that kept leaping straight from the tree into our mouths. After an hour we had both nearly filled our buckets, so reconvened at ground level to take stock. There was still so much fruit on the tree we couldn't possibly strip it bare even if we'd wanted to, but we decided after a water break taken stretched out in the long grass, to at least top up our buckets and leave the rest of the fruit for the birds and bugs to devour. After another thirty minutes of work we were done and had collected probably not far short of 30 kilos of cherries. They looked beautiful en masse, dark and shiny with a few bright green leaves and stalks still attached due to our clumsy picking techniques. We reloaded the car and made our way back home, ready for the real work.

The first thing we did with the cherries was put them in the cool of the pantry while we contacted Sandor for him to collect what he wanted of them. At lunchtime, he popped round to see us in his lunch break, looking genuinely happy at our haul and that the fruit had not been abandoned to rot on the tree. We tried to offload a whole bucket of fruit on him, but he settled for a large bagful and wandered back to work, popping cherries in his mouth as he went. We set to work that afternoon adding some fruit and sugar to bottles of vodka to steep slowly for months in preparation for a tasty Christmas liqueur. We then set aside a few kilos for bottling - filling sterilised glass jars with washed whole fruit, covering the fruit with sugar water, gently screwing on the lids and then placing the full jars in a boiling water bath for 20 minutes or so. The lids eventually seal tightly shut and the jars, in a similar way to canning, should be completely sealed and able to last for several years in a cool dark place. We were happy with the day's work. The buckets were slowly emptying, but we were still left with a copious amount of fruit. Not helped by the fact that Sandor dropped in to see us again that evening to return the majority of the fruit he had taken at lunchtime, saying that he 'didn't need it'. We suspected that this was almost certainly a message from his long-suffering wife, who we imagined, on being handed the bag, rolled her eyes and made her unwillingness to process the fruit very clear indeed. And so the buckets were topped up again.

The next couple of days were largely cherry-based and quite exhausting. After hooking out some of the most delicious looking for the fruit-bowl, we had decided to use the remaining cherries for wine and jam, and to dry several kilos in the hot summer sun. Unfortunately, this meant that they all had to be de-stoned ... which in turn meant hours hunched over bowls and buckets, Joe using an ingenious metal cherry-pitter and me using my thumbs to prize apart the cherry while scooping out the stone with a finger. It was a sure-fire way to get a tight neck and shoulders and to ruin whatever clothes we were wearing with splashes and drips of super-staining cherry juice. Then there were the maggots. We discovered quickly that the ripest of the cherries each seemed to house a single maggot, snuggled and squirming around the centre as if in its very own cosy womb. This was pretty off-putting considering how many cherries we'd already eaten - just popping the fruit into our mouths and spitting out the pits as we worked. We'd probably just upped our protein levels significantly. I struggled to get my head around this conundrum. Such delicious fruit, contaminated with such ugly little beasties. We consoled ourselves with the fact that the firmest of the cherries - the ones we were favouring to eat fresh - tended to be maggot-free ... but I still can't eat a cherry to this day without first breaking it open and removing the pit (and whatever else might be in there). So the cherry pitting task quickly became a cherry pit and maggot removal task. I am so vehemently against food wastage - a trait that I had instilled in me at a very young age - that throwing all these kilos of fruit away was simply never an option. It didn't take me long at all to toughen up to maggot removal. Just as in the garden I've had to get used to picking up slugs and worms with my bare hands and become accustomed to removing bees, wasps and

spiders from the house, so here I was soon scooping stone and maggot up and with a deft flick of
the finger depositing them in the compost
bucket. Sometimes if a job needs doing, you just
have to do it - no amount of complaining or dis-
gust gets it done any quicker. And with this phil-
osophy, we soon had a huge vat of cherry flesh to
stew up with equal amounts of sugar for numerous jars of jam and a fermenting bucket full of
fruit ready for water, sugar and yeast for cherry
wine. The remaining cherries were spread thinly
across a vast net curtain over several pallets in
the garden to dry, which would take about a
week if the sun remained hot enough.

It seemed that no sooner had we processed Sandor's bucketloads of fruit and wiped the sticky
juice from our brow, happy not to see another
cherry stone (or maggot) for another year than
Tamas was standing at the gate smiling and
smoking, ringing vigorously on the gate bell and
shouting "mit csinalsz?" ("what are you doing?")
which is his subtle way of saying "hey, you look
like you're not doing anything important". They
had a very tall cherry tree full of fruit and wondered if we could help, what with both Tamas
and Margit not being either the age nor physical
build conducive to clambering up tall trees. Joe
and I looked at each other knowingly, with just
a tinge of reluctance, but nevertheless agreed
and we were soon stood in their garden receiv-

ing our instructions. Joe was sent as high as he could manage with a bucket and meat hook on which to hang it in the branches, while I was allowed to work using a small ladder, with orders not to touch the really low fruit that was being saved for their young grandson to pick on his weekend visit. So with just a twinge of deja vu, there was Joe, working diligently in the topmost branches 20 feet above my head, absentmindedly dropping rotten fruit and other debris on me like a mischievous monkey as I worked below. Tamas helped, leaning another ladder precariously against the tree trunk, but Margit found it all a little too much, occasionally coming out to watch the higher boughs of the tree bouncing and cracking, looking scared that she may suddenly become partly responsible for a broken Englishman in her garden. But the morning passed accident-free - and a pleasant hour or so of picking and practising our rusty Hunglish later, we had emptied the tree well enough. The fruit was shared across three buckets, two of which were handed straight to me and Joe to go home with, despite our protests that they should give some to their family. But they wouldn't hear of it, so off we went ... to make another big batch of cherry wine, the fastest way of using such a huge amount of fruit.

June's not just about cherries though - all going well, it marks the start of our regular harvesting in the garden, and sudden expansion in culinary activity. The strawberries, raspberries and salad leaves continue in abundance. We have so many rows of radish ready that, aside from throwing them into our salads and chomping on them as snacks, we slice and ferment them in jars of lightly salted water, which turns them into a sour, pickly preserve to be used at a less radishy time of the year. We've even used the leafy radish tops to make pesto - blitzing them together with toasted sunflower seeds, oil, salt and lemon to create a nutritious and tasty spread. After weeks of carefully watching out for the humbug-looking colorado beetles amongst the foliage of the potato patch, we are now able to dig for the treasure of baby potatoes. These 'earlies' are small, slightly waxy and totally delicious - we get through bowls of them as simple potato salad from June onwards, just boiled with a sprinkling of chopped chives, salt and pepper. There are plenty of beetroots ready to boil, cool and serve with some chopped dill and balsamic vinegar and the first rows of carrots are ready at the same time as the kohl-rabi and summer cabbage - perfect timing to throw together for some beautifully crunchy coleslaws. Every few mornings I wander around the garden with a tray to pluck the flower heads from the divine smelling chamomile bushes, then leave them to dry in the sun so that they can be stored for tea throughout the year. The garlic and onions by now are looking plump and their leaves starting to flop and fold, a sign that they are ready to lift. They spend a few days in the sun on the warm concrete at the front of the house until their outer skin is dry and flaky, then I enjoy a leisurely few hours plaiting them together into meter-long strings, ready to hang for further drying and then storage in the pantry. The garden is looking wonderfully colourful now too, despite us spending next to nothing on flowers. Our chrysanthemums won't flower until early autumn, but they are lush and bushy having been divided from one 'mother plant' the previous autumn. We have marigolds blooming everywhere, from borders to actual rows amongst the veg plots, all from seed saved from the previous year. The sunflowers, also from last year's seed are monstrously tall and proudly showing off massive golden heads, although they look nothing as spectacular in such a small number compared to the fields of them around the villages at this time of year. There are nasturtiums of various colours, the leaves and petals both great to throw into salads for a peppery flavour and cornflowers, poppies, alyssum, climbing ipomoea, nigella and chamomile all blooming from seeds that were collected from the garden, or on dog-walks around the village last year. There are terracotta pots of geraniums flowering in bold pink and red, grown from cuttings over winter and placed around the porch and tiny house. All of the flowers are covered in a varied range of insects busying themselves, whether its collecting pollen, eating aphids or simply sunbathing, they're all crucial to our garden's lively little ecosystem.

We'll likely find ourselves at Tamas and Margit's field a couple of times in June. Early on in the month its to help plant hundreds of paprika - a massive crop for them and so important to most Hungarians' national identity. There are a few different varieties, but Tamas grows mainly the 'eros' (strong), 'edes' (sweet) and a small amount of chilli paprika, which are unsurprisingly the hottest type. We weren't too sure what we were helping with, but the vast scale on which we were planting suggested that they would be the bright scarlet paprika that hang outside Hungarian houses to dry in autumn, later to be made into powdered paprika for cooking. As always it was bright and early when we drove up to their field where we met them, the boot of their old car was open revealing crate upon crate of young paprika plants, grown in the small polytunnel in his garden. Tamas, being the diligent worker he is, had already prepared perfectly spaced holes in the ground across the entirety of the field and had barrels of water lined up ready to fill the waiting watering cans. The four of us began planting, following Tamas' tried and tested process - he and Joe would work their way down a row of holes, watering each of them liberally, while Margit and I followed with a handful of plants, prizing two or three decent sized stems from the clump, placing them in the watered hole and covering them with earth. I thoroughly enjoyed this work, made so easy by Tamas' preparation, that I felt that I was just getting into the swing of things when the well-oiled machine was called to a halt. But nothing was wrong, it was just time for a beer break. It was about 7.30 am. As Tamas and Margit were virtually teetotal (with the exception of being lead astray at New Years celebrations, obviously) it turned out that the beer break was mainly for the benefit of Joe and me, another of the many examples of our neighbours looking after us. But they seemed to enjoy the 10-minute breather, Margit fanning herself with her gloves as we swilled down our cup of beer and readied ourselves to finish the planting.

We were done and dusted and home again in no time - both Tamas and Margit seemed very grateful for the help, which perhaps cut a couple of hours off of their morning's task. We were rewarded with a bucket of paprika seedlings that were leftover and while milling around the garden looking for possible spaces for this newly acquired crop, Tamas also dropped over a couple of bags of frozen veggies for us. We really are very spoiled! There was no bribery necessary to get us back in the fields at the end of the month, pulling up semi-dry pea plants and removing the pods as the crop had come to an end, but despite this, we still came away with several kilos of pea pods. We spent the following evenings watching a few films, large glasses of sparkling elderflower fizzing next to us, popping peas from their pods ready to dry out in the sun the next day. Not a bad way to spend an evening.

Perhaps the toughest, or sweatiest at least, neighbourly assistance provided this month was the hay collection with Sandor. He had kindly offered us the latest batch of dried cut grass from the fields next to his house, and it's always helpful to have an ongoing supply at our little homestead. Over the years we've kept a few bales on hand for use as animal bedding, but some has been chopped and thrown into our cobb mixes for fixing walls and it's regularly used from late autumn to mound around the leeks and some other over-wintering veggies and plants that might need a protection blanket from frosts. Anyway, it's always an adventure working with Sandor and more than anything we were looking forward to a few hours loading the fancy new baling machine that he had acquired and watching it spit out beautiful bundles of neatly tied hay. Surely it had to be easier than the previous occasions we've gathered hay, where the only tools available were old rakes and pitchforks apparently from the 1800s. But as per usual, our dealings with Sandor were never quite that simple. First came the preparation - Joe and I raking the pre-cut and dried hay into tidy lines for the machine to pick up - which took a fair bit of time and effort, particularly on a hot Sunday afternoon, the only time that Sandor seemed to have free. We diligently raked our way through the whole field, flecks of straw and dust sticking to our sweaty, sun-creamed skin while Sandor tinkered lovingly with his machine. He fired up the tractor and drove it slowly and carefully down the first line of raked hay so that the machine could scrape it up for processing. But what happened was that the machine being towed behind the tractor picked up the hay, chewed it around its big metal teeth for a few moments and then spewed it out of its rear in a haphazard mess. There were no bales, nor neat lines of hay, just particles of dry grass floating around in the air and a flustered looking Sandor jumping from the cab of the tractor to mutter and tinker a little more with his beloved machine. It seemed that the string tying mechanism was defunct ... and the longer the tinkering in the 40-degree heat, the more hot and bothered we were all becoming. Having been working in the sun for several hours already and with no indication of when Sandor might either fix the machine, or give up on fixing the machine, I decided to take myself off home to catch up on our own chores involving no malfunctioning equipment while Joe, the more patient when it came to Sandor's antics, stayed on to help. About two hours later I found myself opening up the garden gates to allow for our first delivery of hay. Sandor, sweating and dirty in an old baggy vest was driving a loud, sputtering, two-wheeled mini-tractor attached to a trailer that was piled high with the messiest 'bales' of hay I'd ever seen. It seemed that they had just about got the machine to work, albeit not particularly efficiently. Spread-eagled across the top of the hay was Joe with a grin across his face, trying his best to keep the hay from falling off and blowing across the whole of the village - it really was the most ridiculous scene. This palaver was re-peated a further two times, until four or five hours later we had accumulated a massive amount of hay, loosely stacked up and then covered with a tarpaulin in an area of the garden we had recently cleared ready for a new seating area. Our new patio would have to wait ... but at least we wouldn't have to be collecting any more hay for quite some time!

*****

June may well sound busy, but the month brought another pair of Workaway guests to share the load. A young German couple trav-elling through Hungary and particularly inter-ested in alternative lifestyles. We introduced them to our alternative lifestyle by having them chopping and trimming piles of old tree prunings into fire sized sticks, cleaning and tidying our now animal-free sheds, taking over some regular garden duties like mowing, weeding and watering and helping us finish our new cobb pizza oven. This pizza oven was turning into quite the work of art - with a big solid base constructed of spare bricks and donated concrete and a beautifully spherical mud structure growing from the base's surface, we were optimistic about it being a working oven in no time. This despite the slight set back of the mud dome collapsing in on itself once from its own weight - not really surprising given than its only support was the papier mache mould that I had made using our inflated swiss-ball over winter! But we soon had it resculpted by making tennis-balls size mud-bricks and creating a small igloo-like building, complete with little tunnel entrance and metal chimney to lead out the smoke. We spent several fun afternoons making up the cobb mixture from mud dug out from the chicken run, sand, straw and water, stomping it with our bare feet to a smooth paste, a technique mastered the previous autumn when we came to fixing a large crack that had developed in our back mud-wall. Once the structure of the pizza-fire dome was sound, our helpers spent a while building it up and smoothing it over with a wet mud slip - resulting in an obscure scene that was not unlike a comedic version of the iconic pottery scene from 'Ghost' - with less sex and the added bonus of the occasional aroma of chicken shit. But the smell ebbed away and after they had finished we lit a small fire - the first of several - to start drying the structure from the inside. With another good day's work under their belt, our Workawayers washed themselves down and took themselves off to the Tiny House for a few hours relaxation before dinner.

Joe and I were so pleased that our little Tiny House was getting some good use. We thought it was a really cute little space, created on the cheap with mostly donated pallet wood, providing a double bed at a slightly higher level than normal (reached by a couple of wooden steps) with a mini-lounge space underneath the bed. We decorated it in the shabby chic style that tended to suit our ramshackle homestead - with cheap Persian rugs covering the concrete floor and fabric swathed from the ceiling - both sourced second hand from the neighbouring flea-market village of Ozora. In addition to the rugs and decorated ceiling, we had cushions, pictures, a beautiful oval mirror, candles and books - chosen to especially appeal to our travelling Workaway and Warmshowers guests. It was really quite pretty and homely, if small, and as it sat directly in front of our own house, we could see the cosy glow of head torches from the windows at night and we hoped that our guests were as comfy as we were when we first tried it out.

The final day with our German Workawayers was a free day for them, but between relaxing and packing up their gear they agreed to come on a last dog walk with us, to a village about 10 minutes drive away, which had a particularly pretty looped walk across rolling vine-covered hills. It was, of course, another beautifully sunny day as we jumped into the car and set off on the short drive, admiring an expanse of blue sky stretched over the village rooftops. What we noticed when we pulled up to park, however, was that a ridge of cloud had just appeared on the horizon just beyond the hills, looking like a muddy-black mountain range. We had a chat and decided between us that we would take the risk of continuing with our plans, thinking that we could easily outwalk the distant lumbering clouds. There were numerous occasions over summer that we would see wicked summer storms approaching - the massive skies split perfectly in two with half a delicate baby blue and the other half an ominous black - but often they would skirt around us, so we were used to paying little attention until the wind picked up and it was obvious we'd get hit. We were about half-way through our walk, though, when it became clear that the clouds had stepped on the gas and were suddenly looming incredibly close. And then there was the wind - the telltale sign. There was nothing that we could do, being mid-way through our circular walk, except to pick up the pace and get back to the car as quickly as we could. The thunder was rumbling angrily and a few flashes of lightning could be seen a fair distance away when I felt the first heavy droplet of rain hit the peak of my cap. We looked at each other and could do nothing but grin maniacally as we knew what we were in for - we had just short of a kilometre to still cover. It had become unnaturally dark when all of a sudden the skies opened and we all simultaneously felt the bucketloads of water hitting us. Sheltering under trees wasn't advisable even though the lightning wasn't too close, so we battled on, heads down and shoulders hunched against the battering rain which at least was strangely warm. The giggling had stopped as the concentration ramped up - we were all soaked to the skin, including Penfold. I made a joking observation that the only part of me untouched by rain was my septum, sheltered as it was by my bowed head, peaked cap and nose ... but only seconds later a droplet leaked through my drenched cap, rolled down my brow and instead of dripping from my nose-tip, it continued to roll carefully underneath it. There was not a single part of me not wet - I shouldn't have spoken so soon! We made it back to the car pretty quickly and bundled in, fortunately not too cold given the time of year, but nevertheless the car steamed up as we set off back to the house. Perhaps even more ridiculous than four adults looking like they'd all been swimming in their clothes, was the fact that on the drive home we overtook the storm and hurriedly got back to the garden where it was still sunny and dry. We were able to close up the Tiny House door, unpeg a few now dry towels from the line and make it inside the house before it caught up with us again, the lightning now blindingly close and the thunder over the house loud enough to vibrate our bones. As towels were handed out and the kettle filled for hot drinks, the rain hit with a ferocity that was deafening and the garden was awash within minutes. But in true Hungarian storm style, by the time our coffee was finished, the drama was subsiding, the rainwater draining and the sun starting to reappear. Within 30 minutes there was very little sign of what had just happened ... other than four full sets of adult clothing pegged out on the line to dry.

Hungarian Cherry Soup

Joe and I first came across this warm sweet soup on our second trip to Hungary. We were taking time out from viewing properties to warm up and refuel with an impossibly cheap lunchtime set menu - sour cherry soup was the starter. It's not something that we ever would have chosen ourselves, but when our bowls of steaming pink soup arrived, the taste of spiced strudel filling put an instant smile on our faces.

Fresh cherries aren't always the most affordable fruit if you don't happen to have access to kilos of them from your garden as we do throughout June, but fortunately a can or jar will work well in this recipe and, in fact, I tend to make this soup out of season with our own bottle cherries which are the same consistency as the canned ones.

ingredients:
2 cups fresh or 1 can cherries
½ cup water
1 cup oat milk
½ tsp vanilla essence
½ tsp cinnamon
¼ cup sugar

Wash and stone the fresh cherries. Add the fruit

to a pan with the water and heat to a gentle boil - simmer until cherries are soft. Stir in the sugar, spice and vanilla. Take the pan off the heat and blitz the soup with a stick blender until smooth. Return the pan to a gentle heat and stir in the oat milk for a minute or two.

This soup is just as delicious served hot or cold and makes for an interesting starter or more classic dessert. You can, of course, un-vegan this dish by using milk or single cream in place of the oat milk and even stir through some sour cream at the end to make it all the more creamy and decadent.

CHAPTER THIRTEEN

Summer/Autumn 2018

The house next door and other eventualities

The sign had been there for a while. Just a smallish square of thin chipboard, tag-tied to the slightly crooked, rusting gate; it had dog-eared corners and a handwritten phone number scrawled next to the announcement 'ELADO'. We would wander past the house fairly regularly on dog walks - on the short village loop past the giant stork nest, up the hill from which you could just make out our home and down again past 'walnuts', the little overgrown track that in autumn was an absolute treasure trove for wal-nut foraging. We didn't at first make much of this house that was for sale. There are lots of houses, in lots of villages throughout Hungary that have similar handmade signs attached to their gates, all in varying stages of loneliness and dilapida-tion. Signs of the times. The only difference was that this one was right next to ours, the two gardens only separated by a long stretch of unruly hedgerow. There would be occasions when I would swing in the hammock under our apple tree next to this hedge and daydream about owning that big, empty garden next to ours. I would imagine a hidden passage cut through the foliage, like an enchanted pathway to a rural Narnia, overrun with fruit and flowers and fauns ... the opportunities seemed limitless! On one particular dog walk, when Joe had foolishly decided to stay at home, I was overcome with a romantic notion to buy the place, knowing that it would be incredibly cheap and presuming that it would prove useful in one way or another. I liked the idea of doing the house up cheaply - simple whitewashed walls, a second-hand wood-burner, some rugs and candles, no internet and perhaps not even electricity; herbs growing right outside the door and a garden full of vegetables. We could market it as a detox retreat for those who needed a break from their stressful, hectic daily lives. 'Come to rural Hungary - eat food straight from the garden, read a book in the shade of a cherry tree, turn off the news and social media and lay on the grass in the sun, doing absolutely nothing'. I had it all worked out. I could see it so clearly. I even saw the big expanse of garden in autumn full of tall corn stems, cut into a simple maze to amuse the village kids at Halloween for a few Forints entrance fee. The further I walked, the more ideas I came up with, and the more ideas I came up with, the more excited I got about getting home and pitching my thoughts to Joe ...

'Mmmmmm. That's a shit idea' responded Joe without hesitation and with complete disregard for my child-like excitement and enthusiasm. He went on to explain, listing the costs, risks and simple lack of demand for a niche bed and breakfast in the middle of nowhere. He was right. I knew it was just a pipe dream really. Of all the places in the world that people could go to relax and escape, why would they choose our unknown, unkempt village? The costs of maintaining the place would probably outweigh any income. And we were kept busy enough really just looking after ourselves. It was nice while it lasted, but I had to let the daydream go ... life quickly resumed to normal as we resumed tending to our own little homestead.

It was with some reluctance and just a slight pang of regret that some six months later, when Joe's folks were visiting, I mentioned that the house next door happened to be for sale, playfully adding that it would no doubt be going for a song. I had a sneaking feeling that it would pique their interest, particularly as they seemed to be growing frustrated with work and weary of the general franticness of life back in the UK. Although I would no longer be able to imagine the house becoming my own little rustic money-making project, I knew it had been for sale for well over a year and at least now its full potential could be realised. So in what seemed to be a heartbeat, we found ourselves greeting the owner, having arranged a viewing through a helpful Hungarian friend that I had serendipitously met in Brazil 10 years earlier. As soon as we walked through the gate the house and garden seemed to morph into something well beyond my expectations. There was a good amount of land that just seemed to expand further in size as you wandered into it; A big cherry tree, a peach tree, small apple, pear and plum trees, numerous hazels, and a ridiculous amount of raspberry bushes. The garden was all grass which was in poor condition, but it provided a beautifully blank canvas. Hidden beneath a cluster of hazels was a well with a hand pump, and alongside the main house was a cellar and numerous ramshackle outhouses. The house itself seemed structurally sound with just a few cracks and crumbling surfaces typical of an old adobe building, and it had new double glazing, gas heaters and a huge water tank. It was a small house but the three main rooms were bright and spacious, with beautiful wooden floors in two rooms and smart tiling in what seemed to have been the kitchen. We mooched and poked around as much as we could without being rude, asking questions in our limited Hungarian and smiling at the owner who seemed ecstatic to be finally showing people around. It was clear by the time we left that we would shortly be asking my Hungarian friend to get involved in some negotiations. There wasn't too much negotiating, in fact, to reduce the price from around the £10,000 mark to just £6,000 and suddenly we were contacting a lawyer to sort out payment and legalities. Well! Where did that come from? Joe's folks had arrived with their suitcases for a short holiday and left a week later with a house and future plans of long Hungarian homesteading summers. It only took a further few weeks (and a month since viewing the property) to have the new keys sitting on our coffee table, with myself and Joe suddenly wondering what potential impact this change might make on our somewhat idyllic lifestyle that we'd taken time to foster. After an initial panic, we quickly concluded that it was most definitely a good thing. Good for their health and happiness, and our own company, great to have extra land to grow on and, during their six month stints in Hungary, there was the added bonus of enabling us some freedom to escape for weeks or even months at a time to travel without worrying that the garden and animals wouldn't be tended to.

The first and most important task for us as temporary caretakers of this new land was to create some easy access. Although the gardens were adjacent to each other, it took a walk around the block via the main road to the front gate, a setup that simply wasn't convenient enough for us if we were to be checking mail, picking fruit and using the cellar on a regular basis. Joe rectified this situation one morning by simply grabbing some shears and hacking a human-sized hole through the deep tangle of hedge in the bottom corner of our garden. He then, with a spade and various scraps of wood and brick, created some fairly decent steps to tackle the height drop between the two gardens. Within a couple of days, we had the rustic garden passageway that I had imagined the year before and a way to easily reach the mass of huge, ripening raspberries that I had been recently eyeing through the gaps in the hedgerow. By the month's end we had done a thorough litter pick of the long-abandoned garden, trimmed the front hedge and mowed the lawn several times, spent hours raking the old matted grass that had created a thatch-like cover over the entire lawn area, picked, jammed and gorged ourselves on kilos worth of raspberries, planted some spare tomato seedlings in holes dug out of the turf, discovered a gooseberry bush and sweet chestnut tree, created a herb garden, formed a giant compost heap, fixed the crooked gate and re-aligned some of the leaking house tiles. The extra garden was a fantastic empty playground for Penfold, who was able to hone his football and frisbee catching skills on the huge expanse of lawn, in addition to making friends with his new loud and barky canine neighbours, by being equally loud and barky. We did have good intentions of working on the house a little - perhaps some cement work and plastering, getting the bathroom in working order - but it became clear quite early on that we couldn't commit to doing as much as we had wanted to with both houses and gardens; and also, we had to remember that this wasn't actually our house and we should probably leave it to the owners to make their mark rather than us! With the help of our wonderful Workaway guests, we simply did a deep-clean of the kitchen and bathrooms, painted the dark, creepy cellar so that it felt a little less cave-like and continued working on the garden - regularly mowing the grass and starting to rotivate, dig and weed a large rectangular patch of land in preparation for planting double our crops the following year. It turned out to be an epic task, the top layer of grass was thick and matted with clover and thatch, the soil was compacted and the grass rhizomes had created a super-strong network under the soil that prevented us from easily turning over the earth and picking out the bindweed. After just an hour or two of work, we were guaranteed to be sweating buckets and have our hands filthy, cut and calloused from trying to pull out these tenacious roots.

By the end of summer, the digging and weeding slowed to a halt once the new veg plot had expanded to about the size of a tennis court. There was still plenty of room to expand it further depending on how the first year of growing went, after which we could reassess and extend if necessary, but for now, we were satisfied and excited at its potential. It wasn't long at all until we started using our new space - planting long rows of onion sets and soon having regimental lines of green shoots standing to attention from the otherwise brown earth. As the temperature cooled and the days shortened we decided to plant an autumn salad crop, the first time we'd tried sowing anything other onion and garlic outside of our usual springtime sowing window. We were keen to try extending our growing season and decided that with the weather now so similar to spring, there was a good chance for success. And success there was. A short while after planting our left-over packets of rocket, radish, spinach and lettuce seeds we were harvesting an abundance of fresh salad normally unavailable to us at this time of year. We had such a bumper crop of radishes that we gave bunches away to both Sandor and our neighbours and still had enough to slice and ferment into jars of pickly goodness. The cellar quickly proved its worth too, providing a cooler overflow space for our chutneys, boxed apples, numerous cured squash and buckets of oversized beet from next-door's garden.

*****

After a breakfast of toasted fruit bread slathered in apple butter, we head out for a walk with Penfold before the day warms up too much. Next door we see Margit raking up the first of the fallen leaves and admire their strings of bright scarlet paprika hung up to dry in long garlands like a theatre curtain across the front of the house; we bump into Sandor, already filthy from whatever early morning chores he's been up to, and then sneak up the overgrown path between his house and the bakery that leads to the tracks along the vineyards and wine cellars behind the village. Penfold is unclipped and bounces off ahead down the narrow grass fringed trail, enjoying his freedom, fresh air and fox poo. This is his time. And seeing him with a wide grin and his tongue lolling, thoroughly absorbed in his mooching, warms my heart and makes me so happy - both he and I, at this moment, have not a care in the world. Joe and I walk side by side once on the wider vineyard tracks, sometimes putting the world to rights, but often in silence on sensory overload, indulging in the free stuff nature has to offer. There is gentle sunshine, but a cool breeze that smells so fresh and clean, the sky is a soft blue, pretty against the different shades of green in the undergrowth and it is peaceful, with just the bird call and corn leaves rustling. I mean no disparagement when I say that there is no stand out scenery in our village. We revel in the simplicity of the dust track with its bordering fields of dry corn and sunflowers and little hobbit-like cellar buildings. As the trail takes us up a gentle incline, we have a pleasant view of terracotta rooftops set among bushy gardens, the two church spires at either end of the village and some dusky rolling hills way over in the neighbouring county. Whether 20 minutes or over an hour, our walks are never rushed and this time becomes a valuable body and mind reset, when everything is good in the world. On our return journey, before we cross the rickety, patched up wooden bridge over the stream, I spot some walnuts on the floor. It's a little early for them, but they look big and I can't possibly leave them. I roll them under my foot to remove their sticky green and black cases and put the nuts in my pocket - it seems that the autumn foraging has already begun. We call Penfold from his pheasant tracking in the undergrowth, clip his lead back on and he guides us back up the narrow path on the familiar route home.

Back at the house, Joe gets the coffee-pot stoked up while I kick off my shoes and wander around the garden barefoot after first letting the chooks out of their run to free range for a few hours. I tread carefully along the grassy path between vegetable patches, cautious of slugs and chicken poo, and as I pass between the brassica plots I can hear the pitter patter of flea beetles scattering out of my way. These pests have, in the space of a week, turned our luscious green Chinese cabbages into the most delicate brown lace, and are working on the rest of our cabbages too. We've tried various natural concoctions of chilli and mint teas watered over the crop, but nothing has helped and it's a little bit heart-breaking. But we hold some hope that when the weather turns, the bugs will disperse and the plants will make a come-back. 'Stranger things have happened', I sigh to myself. I pick some lonely looking green tomatoes from our remaining dried plants and pull the rest up, with the exception of a plant that has numerous little green babies and more flowers. This plant has been responsible for some of our most delicious pasta sauces this summer, so why not see if we can stretch it out. The aubergine and pepper plants are loaded with goodies and the squash and pumpkin plants have, in the last week or so suddenly been spreading wildly, like its now their time to shine. Their yellow flowers are big and bold against the rambling, bushy leaves and the squash that we have are hidden well ... but we've been treasure hunting over the past weeks and we know where they all are, sitting patiently and swelling, in preparation for our winter soups, risottos, curries and pies. The leeks are looking strong and we have more parsnips than any other year so far if the leafy tops are anything to go by, which will make up for the weedy little carrot crop that we're having. I take a bucket and pick a few bunches of purple grapes for some juice with lunch. We haven't the inclination to make wine from our modest crop of wine grapes, but the daily fruit juice has been like ambrosia for the taste buds, so sweet and flavoursome that it has to be diluted. I wash the fruit under water from the outdoor tap, drain it, then take a seat on the porch step in the sun with the bucket between my legs - then I hand squeeze the grapes. We have a press, but it takes time to set up, time to clean and there are only a few bunches of grapes anyway. And besides, I like the way the grapes pop when I squeeze them and how the skins slime between my fingers. I notice something on my t-shirt. A grape pip? I take time to gently pick it up and look at it properly - it's a tiny reverse ladybug, black with two red spots. Apparently also called the 'twice-stabbed ladybug'. Sometimes it's nice to notice the little things. Literally. Joe hollers that coffee is ready, so we reconvene in the conservatory, on the oversized couch seats donated by Tamas a month ago. The conservatory has come into its own now that we have comfy chairs - also known as the 'thinking chairs' since they were the location of Joe's recent nightly chess matches with one of our Workaway guests. It's the perfect spot to curl up with a drink and a book; or to sit and absorb the garden with a cat on your lap; or to take cover in a summer storm, with the lightening in full view, the thunder on full volume and a torrent of rainwater running past your feet. We're excited for autumn when we'll be able to use it more often with cooler temperatures not turning the small space into walk-in oven.

With coffee drunk, I spend a few minutes making bread for lunch - flour, water, yeast, salt, sugar, a quick knead - and leave it in the tin to prove on the kitchen table while I make a rare call home to England to catch up on family news. I head back outside into the daylight again once the bread is in the oven. Our first pumpkin is curing in the sun on the porch, together with a tray of shelled cobnuts, some remaining slices of tomato and a huge sunflower head. I collect a basket and wander down to the end of the garden, feeling like the pied piper as Fergus, Blondie and Marley, our three female cats, follow me across to the compost in the furthermost corner and down the slightly precarious home-made steps through the hedge to the 'other' garden. I'm here to pick tomatoes that we planted a few months back before the slugs hollow them out, and also to gather cobnuts that have started to fall in abundance. Cobnuts are pretty much hazelnuts but a little bigger and longer in shape. The tree itself is the same and there are several of them in the other garden, all laden with nuts. I move at a steady pace, positioning my basket and crouching to greedily gather all the nuts within reach that are earwig-hole free without adding any hapless creepy crawlies into the basket with them. I can hear the nuts falling around me as I'm gathering them, proof that they're ready. The cats are stalking each other through the tall grass nearby and I sit and spy on them for a while as they bop each other on the head and roll around play-fighting, before realising they're being watched and running to me for some attention. I probably have a couple of kilos of these glossy shelled nuts, which at the moment are at various stages of pale green to light brown as they ripen and dry. We lay them out in the sun until we get around to shelling them, then we lay them out in the sun a bit more. Once dry enough they're stored in jars in the pantry with a sprinkling of rice in the hope it will keep them moisture free. These jars of nuts are an absolute boon for self sufficient vegans! They get blitzed into various pestos, soaked and fermented into cheese, toasted and made into a 'nutella' style spread and are great for adding to cakes, salads, muesli and for casual snacking. The cobnuts are added to the growing collection of goodies mounting up in the pantry - we have jars of sundried tomatoes, apple butter and thanks to a fantastic book on fermentation for my birthday, we also have several jars of sauerkraut, some fermented salted pears, carrots, spiced beetroot, mixed herbs, vine leaves and ginger. The experimentation continues, but one of my favourites so far is the fermented chopped mixed herbs. The leaves lose some bitterness, gain some tanginess (plus lots of beneficial bacteria for your gut) and when blitzed together with cobnuts and garlic make a lovely pesto. This was lunch today ... just some freshly made pesto smeared on the freshly baked bread. Simple.

After lunch, the breeze has picked up and mountainous puffed clouds have rolled in as expected so I'm stretched on the sofa writing. Joe's doing the washing up outside and has plans to gather some late summer veg and rustle up a tagine for tea. It's still muggy and I'm looking forward to the forecast storms over the next couple of days. A great excuse for some reading in the 'thinking chairs', some Hungarian language practise and some extra yoga. We're waiting for some cooler weather until we embark on some of the more energetic jobs, like stripping and painting the front doors, composting the veg patches and other various maintenance jobs.

It's so good having the luxury of time. It's a great chance to reflect. Looking back over our last three full years in Hungary, we can appreciate how every year has been different, bringing with them assorted challenges and experiences. We've come full circle with our animal ownership for example. Not so long ago the menagerie consisted of chickens, goats, rabbits, cats and a dog, with the best intentions to add a hive of bees and perhaps even a pond or tank full of talapia in an ingenious but no-doubt slightly bodged home-made aquaponics system. But now we're happy and healthy vegans, embracing our not-so-inner hippy and feeling a lot more content and at peace for it. I miss the animals a huge amount, but without an income, appropriate space or, in fact, a need for them, it's the right thing to have moved on. The couple of chickens remaining are now simply pets and the ducks that will be acquired next year will be put to work on slug eradication. None will ever be for the pot. We've found a flow in what we're doing with the garden too. I'm better at rolling with the punches that the seasons may bring and tend not to slump into a childish funk at the loss of a whole crop. We both are more resilient, flexible, imaginative and of course, knowledge-able - with the weather, the crops, our food and in our attempted self sufficient lifestyle in general. Of course we're not 100% self sufficient, I think it's very difficult to achieve that without depriving yourself from some basic pleasures of life. But what we have done is simplify every aspect of our life - reduce our waste, reduce our need for things and therefore our need for so much money. This is a life skill that we hope to take with us to whatever future project we end up on and we're excited at how things might develop from here. Maybe in a different place, with different people - but as our contacts here increase, maybe not. We both feel that some sort of like-minded community might be the way forward for us in the long-term, but we're not sure what that might look like yet.

So what will 2019 bring? For sure there is more land to grow on, which is also more land to look after. But in theory there will be double the people here over the summer months, so we're not too worried about that. We hope that the year will bring new friends, in the shape of Workaway and Warmshowers guests. Being altruistic as far as we can afford to be is incredibly satisfying, not to mention an opportunity to share what we're doing and demonstrate that there are alternative ways of living. We look forward to the freedom afforded to us by Joe's folks being next door and hope to take some of our planned cycle breaks in Spring and Autumn - eco-friendly, low-cost holidays, making good use of our central european base. Scratching that travel itch, but more sustainably. Hopefully the anticipation of those first salad leaves, swelling pea pods and ripening strawberries won't hold us back!

And finally, we know we'll need to make an income at some point as the kitty continues to dwindle. We have ideas. Some of them tend to be pie-in-the-sky, but others may well pan out to be a whole new adventure in self sufficiency and permaculture. It is the future after all.

Herb And Tomato Loaf

What smells better wafting from the kitchen than fresh, home-baked bread?

We make bread a lot - on average probably every other day. It's a cheap and simple staple for breakfast toast, soup dipping, sandwiches or just snacking and can be as versatile as your imagination. It's also very quick. Although proving and baking take time, the actual hands-on time required is probably no more than 10 minutes.

In winter we prove the dough on the top of the bedroom ceramic heater, but in summer we can simply leave the dough in its tin, proving on the kitchen table.

Ingredients:

500g flour - I use a mix of strong bread flour, wholemeal flour and plain white, in roughly equal quantities
a sachet of dried instant yeast
teaspoon sugar
pinch salt
sundried tomatoes
dried mixed herbs
300ml lukewarm water
extra plain flour for dusting hands and table

Measure out the flour and mix all the dry ingredients together in a large mixing bowl. Chop the tomatoes into small pieces to ensure an even distribution and likewise, make sure that the herbs are finely crumbled too. Add to the other ingredients in the bowl. Make a well in the centre and pour in the water.

The mixing and kneading is down to you! If you love to get stuck in and messy, dive in with both hands mixing everything together until fully combined and then, scrape the sticky mixture from your hands, dust them and the table with flour and knead the dough for a few minutes until it's smooth and elastic. If you're not so keen on a mess, a hooked index finger for the first mixing will do the same job until you have that sticky dough ball that you can dust liberally with flour and get to kneading without getting covered in goo.

Place your dough in a greased bread tin or formed into a ball on a tray lined with grease-proof paper, lightly cover with a tea-towel and leave in a warm place for up to an hour to prove, where it should double in size. If it's particularly warm it may rise quickly, so check on it from time to time. Some recipes will call for a second prove, which involves knocking the air out of the dough and letting it rise for a second time. We tend not to do this as we see minimal difference and one prove keeps things simple, at the most, a second prove may make the loaf very slightly lighter.

Once the dough has a nice rise, bake it at a high heat for ten minutes and then reduce the heat for a further 40 minutes. Tip from the tin/tray and cool on a wrack. Don't try to slice the loaf while it's hot, the steam will just ruin the texture, leaving you with squashed, wet crumbed slices of bread.

You can add more or less anything to this basic bread recipe instead of the tomatoes and herbs. Mixed seeds work well as does a generous shake of raisins, a spoon or two extra sugar and some cinnamon for a spiced fruity loaf. You can also shape it in any way you want to, including rolls (reduce the cooking time for rolls).

CHAPTER FOURTEEN

What's in our plots?

In early 2016, the first year that we planted on the entirety of our land, we separated the vegetable plots into manageable sizes either with strategically placed logs or using the natural layout between vines, trees and the paths that we created through the garden. Beside each plot, we placed a brick with a painted number so that we could organize what we were planting and where. In this way, the land felt far less intimidating and we were able to plan our crops and refer to areas of the garden more easily. The painted digits have now eroded away and the bricks have gradually found their way into various structures around the garden, but the plots remain as they were and each year are integral to our planning process.

This is an overview of what we planted in those plots in 2017.

Plot one is located in an isolated spot at the top

of the garden, close to the front gate It's at a high point of the garden, nestled between grapevines and an apple tree and so finds itself sheltered from the worst of the weather, be it frosts or midday summer sun. For this reason, it's quite ideally situated for our small salad patch, sown in early spring and containing an annual variation of rocket, spinach, assorted lettuce, radish and also some chamomile - and is the only plot that we plant with similar crops each year. The leaves from this patch are the first new greens for the year and are gratefully added to salads and sandwiches. The rocket is often incorporated into pesto. The radish, if we have too many to simply eat fresh, we ferment in lightly salted water, sometimes with seasoning, so they turn slightly pickly and last for months. The salad is normally finished by mid-summer unless we let the spinach and rocket continue, but they have a tendency to go to seed in the heat of the summer and we have alternative greens to turn to by this time. This is when the vines can become quite jungly and need trimming, so we use some of the large leaves to make dolmades (stuffed vine-leaves) and add to our pickles to help keep them crunchy. We let the weeds and grass grow on the plot once empty of salad, although we keep them low to the ground by mowing or cutting back with shears, and this is when the chamomile flowers take over. Once it's bloomed we harvest the flower heads and dry them for fragrant herbal tea. After this, the area is empty other than the grapes and apples and available as an overflow plot for any late crops that we want to plant, usually some extra kale.

Plot two is a large triangular area running alongside our top path, exposed to sunshine most of the day, with the exception of the shadow from the tiny house in the mornings. Hungarian paprika took up most of the space in this plot, transplanted as 5-10cm high seedlings from the polytunnel once all chance of frost had passed. We had a good crop of narrow, yellow peppers from July through to October that were picked only when required and used in a variety of meals from salads to curries and goulash, with any excess sliced into csalamade. As we'd planted a lot of peppers here we used the space around the borders for some extra overflow crops - onions, savoy cabbage and tomatoes.

Sandwiched between plot two and the goat paddock is **plot three,** which this particular year was dedicated to our bean crop - red kidney, borlotti, pinto, lima and broad. We decided to grow a large crop of beans as when dried they keep so well, are nutritious and versatile. The broad bean was the only crop that we ate fresh, but it wasn't particularly successful, providing only a few handfuls of beans, perhaps due to a particularly dry spell while they were flowering and our failure to meet their watering needs. The rest of the crops were hardier, planted straight into the ground in May and providing us with kilos of beans from August to October which were sun-dried, jarred and stored in the pantry for use over winter.

Courgettes have been a reliably prolific crop for us and so have **plot four** all to themselves, which was particularly good in 2017 as they had a fair bit of shade from the cherry and apple trees that border the area. We had about eight courgette plants, four green and four yellow - they taste similar but it's nice to have a little colour variation. We try not to let them grow too large, although there are generally a few that go unnoticed for a while, hidden beneath a large leaf, and grow to proportions that the BFG would be proud of. When the crop gets going we can pick several every morning, so it's handy that we love eating them and can throw them into almost every dish that we prepare in summer. Some made their way into batches of preserved tomato passata and we've successfully dried several kilos in the sun once sliced. They have to be vacuum packed for storage but have proved to be a useful addition to stews in winter where they re-hydrate nicely. Courgettes are the only crop that we've been known to give away bags of to friends and neighbours, there are just so many of them!

Plot five is a slim plot tucked between cherry

and apple trees so we have to be a little careful of their roots, not planting anything too close. This year it was a few alternating rows of onions and carrots, two great staples of the vegetable garden that grow well together. We can never have enough onions and carrots and unfortunately haven't been able to provide enough to see us through a whole year, but we had plenty from June through to December. As with most of our vegetables, we dig up what we need only when we need it, so the carrots stay in the ground until autumn and when the frosts set in we dig up and pack any remaining roots in buckets of moist sand. Our early batch of onions, usually red and planted the autumn prior, are ready by mid-summer, so we lift them all, dry them in the sun, plait them and hang them in the pantry when their skins are nicely dried, where they'll last for months if they don't get eaten first! The spring planted crop will be gathered in the same way a few months later.

Next to plot five and taking us nearly to the bottom of our gently sloping garden is **plot six**, a patch planted with peas and mangetout plants in early spring. The mange tout are eaten fresh as soon as they're big enough to harvest, often going straight from plant to mouth as they're so sweet and delicious. The peas come a little later - we might get a few small pickings at first but come June we'll take the whole plants up and have a day or two of picking and podding. We eat a lot fresh, but we make sure that plenty are laid out on trays in the sun to dry before being vacuum packed and stored in the pantry for winter. We did try bottling them in salt water, but the jars only lasted a couple of weeks before they turned into a putrid fermented mess, so we stick with the simple drying now. Not wanting to waste anything edible, occasionally we'll cook up some of the more tender pea pods, which make a very tasty soup. With the plot empty by June we then planted dwarf beans on the plot - several rows of both yellow and green beans which grow fairly fast and can be ready to harvest within six weeks or so.

The above mentioned three plots are all bordered by grape vines, but beside them, there is a long fairly slim area that flanks the garden fence and this is **plot seven**. We planted this plot with sweetcorn in late spring, adding cucumber and squash seeds a little later as they grow well between the corn plants. The cucumbers are the first to provide us with food - just a few plants can provide plenty of small, squat little cucumbers that are so common here in Hungary for fermenting and pickling. We do preserve many of them, especially if we have a slightly bitter tasting crop, but any sweet cucumbers are added to salads throughout the summer months. Our corn has not been hugely successful, but when we do get some good-sized cobs they're normally sweet, juicy and delicious ... we just haven't had many of them and so also haven't had the need for any preserving. The squash come along a lot later, we spot their big beautiful flowers and fruit appearing from summer, but they don't start looking promising until at least the beginning of autumn, depending on the variety. Squash are a great autumn and winter crop because we can grow a fairly large amount, cure them in the sun and they last us through to spring.

At the top end of plot seven we have a decent sized raspberry and strawberry plot, already established before we arrived at the house - we didn't know that the unknown brambles were raspberries until our first spring at the house, but we were really pleased that we had been patient enough to wait and see. On a warm morning, the plot smells sticky sweet with ripe fruit. We pick strawberries and raspberries simultaneously through May and June and had enough for daily breakfasts and some spare for some delicious traditional jams. At the bottom end of the plot, wedged in the very corner of the garden, we have a few large compost troughs constructed from scavenged bricks and pallets. All of our kitchen and garden waste goes on the compost (if it doesn't reach the animals first) and all of the dirty straw from the animal pens gets thrown in too. They remain uncovered so that the air and weather help decomposition, but the pallet walls keep everything contained. We do try to turn them over once a year, but we've also found that if we don't, we still end up with a good quantity of quality compost, it just needs to be dug from beneath the layers of fresher stuff on the top. Close to the compost, along the back fence of the garden is another strawberry plot, below a couple more cherry trees, these were replanted from the original mega-patch when we located the goats there in autumn 2016. It's fairly productive but does get a little overrun with nettles that we have yet to do anything about.

Moving back into the central garden from plot seven is this year's tomato patch on **plot eight.** We got ourselves more organised in 2017, abandoning the rustic freestyle tomato plants of the previous year for structured rows with stakes and wire supports. In all, we had about 40 plants of four different varieties, all grown from seed in our polytunnel and planted out in late spring. This gave us a huge crop that we were able to feast on from July throughout the summer with plenty for sun-drying and cooking into passata, which lasted through to the following April. My particular favourite were the huge, ribbed variety called 'Marmande' - beautifully sweet and juicy, they taste as tomatoes should do when ripened on the vine in the sunshine.

Over the little grass path from the tomatoes is **plot nine** - a long patch that flanks the lower fence of the garden, at the lowest and in spring, the wettest part of the garden. This plot was separated into a few blocks of different crops due to its size - chard, onion, beetroot and leek - all of which grew very well considering the lack of shade during the hot summer months. The chard and beet would wilt terribly in the midday sun, but soon pep up again with their evening watering. Chard is a fantastic addition to our vegetable collection. Similar to spinach in taste and usage, it grows fairly quickly, it's hardy, doesn't succumb to any pests (unless to include pesky free-ranging chickens) and is very versatile to cook with. Leaves and stalks can be added to everything from curries to quiches to cheese scones. It also looks beautiful in the garden as the stems of the 'Bright Lights' variety range through yellow. orange, pink and reds, and the leaves are assorted shades of green. The onions alongside provide a good companion to keep bugs at bay and next to them were our fabulous beetroot, a large and sweet variety called 'Bordo'. We ate them cooked and cooled in salads all summer and pickled several large jars in sweet, spiced vinegar. They lasted in the ground through to late autumn and stored well in the root cellar, but we learned that they began to lose their sweetness the longer they were left in the ground and stored, so in future we'll harvest them when they're at their best, pickling to preserve the flavour. We also ate the beet leaves, choosing the small tender leaves and making sure not to pick too many from each beet - they're packed with nutrition and provide some colour in leafy salads. Finally, at the end of the plot in a block of about 6 rows are our leeks, started off in the polytunnel and replanted when about 10cm in height. As the leeks grow we mound them with earth to encourage sturdy, white stems. We did try an alternative to mounding the year prior - toilet rolls placed around each of the plants - but I can't recommend it, they grew far better with the earth as a support. Our leeks are ready from mid-autumn, in our case, just as our onions were winding down, and lasted through to Christmas. They do well staying in the ground in the cool of early winter, although we know from experience that they're as good as lost once the really heavy frosts move in. They simply can't be dug up in the coldest of temperatures and then turn to slush when they thaw, but fortunately this time around we ate them all before the weather became too bad.

Completing the circuit between plot nine at the bottom of the garden and plot two at the top, lay **plots ten**, **eleven** and **twelve**. They sit alongside a grass and brick-lined pathway dividing the whole area in two and in front of them is the concrete that extends from the front of the house with a trench full of marigolds as a border. **Plot ten** contains our brassicas - summer cabbage, broccoli, cauliflower, savoy cabbage, brussels sprouts and kale. Our broccoli and cauliflower have never grown into what they should be. Unfortunately, we get as far as the leaves and nothing else, which is mildly disappointing, but at least the leaves are tasty. The summer cabbage starts off in the polytunnel in early spring and is transplanted a couple of months later, once the true leaves have just established themselves. We grow a huge number of cabbages because they are so great to preserve into sauerkraut and csalamade which lasts us well into the winter months, as well as being thrown into coleslaws and stir-fries. The kale, Brussels and savoy cabbage are sown straight into the ground in late spring and aren't ready to eat until autumn, but they are a great late crop and the only three things that can last out in the garden through all but the very worst of the cold weather. In a patch next to the brassicas, in **plot eleven,** are our garlic, planted the autumn prior and ready for harvesting by about June. They are pulled up, dried, plaited and hung in the same way as the onions and we can never have enough of them. Even a fairly large and successful crop tends to provide six months worth of bulbs so we are resigned to having to buy them for half of the year. **Plot twelve** holds an array of different root vegetables - carrots, parsnips, turnips and some extra beetroot which are sown directly into the ground and harvested as required. We tend not to have enough turnip or parsnip to have to store them, they simply get eaten in stews, soups and curries.

Across from plot eleven, we have a compact **herb plot** created from a small patch of unconcreted earth beside the house that initially only contained a bush of pretty pale yellow chrysanthemums and some stunning red tulips that remain there still. With some patience, we transformed the plot into a pretty and productive herb garden that provides us with plenty of herbs throughout the year - fresh in summer and autumn, and dried through winter and spring. Sage, mint, oregano, chives and two types of thyme were grown from seed and all thrive from year to year without needing replanting despite the harsh winter temperatures. Mint and lemon balm plants were grown from cuttings from a friend in the village. Parsley is sown annually in any spare space. We have a large pot of rosemary which is brought inside the house during winter due to us losing several plants in our first and second winters. Basil and coriander are grown annually in pots, although the coriander fares much better when sown directly into the ground. In addition to our herb garden we have dill growing like a weed throughout the garden, borage surrounding the outdoor toilet shed and a few extra bushes of thyme, sage, lemon balm and catnip dotted around various borders.

Behind the house is a large, sloping, shady area and home of **plots thirteen** and **fourteen**. We've split these into two due to their scale, planting a decent sized crop of potatoes in plot thirteen, having allowed the baby potatoes to 'chit' or sprout first. They're planted in late April in mounded rows that are positioned across the slope to create a bit of a catchment for rainwater, like an artificial swale. Potatoes enjoy a decent amount of watering and this ensured that any rain (or indeed our hand-watering) would not run immediately to the bottom of the slope and into the neighbour's garden. Once the potato plants grew to about 30cm in height we mounded them up with earth to encourage the tubers to grow and then once more a few weeks later. We had a fantastic crop of decent sized and delicious spuds that we dug up from July onward. Despite various advice to lift and store all of the potatoes by mid-autumn we risked leaving them in the ground until there were any signs of frost as the cool, dark conditions seemed to be suiting them well, with no signs of any pest damage. By mid-November, we decided to dig them up and stored them in a woven sack in the pantry with a heavy towel over them for insulation which kept them in perfect condition until we were ready to eat them. Plot fourteen was simply another space to plant some more of our staple carrot and onions, as before, in alternating rows.

Our **polytunnel** consists of a low arched frame covered with clear sheet plastic which shelters a 'U' shaped raised bed made from spare bricks and earth taken from around the garden, with some added home compost. In early spring we sow rows of cabbage, celery, paprika, chillies, leeks and a few weeks later our tomatoes. Most of the seedlings are pricked out and planted into the plots when sturdy enough, but we leave the celery in place as it seems to grow well in a tight cluster. We did try leaving a selection of brassicas too, to see how they fared through winter in a higher, segregated area of the garden, but on noticing no difference between them and those in plot ten, we won't bother doing this again and instead will transform the area into temporary flower beds.

In addition to our plots, we have quite a few fruit trees. Five apples, five cherry and one each of plum, peach, pear and apricot. The peach has self-seeded and we have re-positioned five more saplings around the garden. We eat as much fruit as we can fresh from the trees, but much of the excess is turned into jam. The cherries are the most versatile - we make some into jam, add some to vodka for a cherry liqueur, stone and dry many to use in baking and a huge quantity goes into cherry wine, together with cherries that our friends and neighbours have allowed us to pick from their land. The apples store well when wrapped individually in paper, lasting through to late winter; but they also make a wonderful spiced apple butter. We've planted a hazel sapling but don't expect any nuts for several years yet, while it matures. On the borders of the garden are several elderflower trees - the blossom makes a fragrant cordial and sparkling wine and the dark berries are also great for wine later in the year. We have a large walnut tree that towers over our sheds from a neighbour's garden and so can pick up any windfall nuts, although we get the majority of our walnuts from various trees around the village.

Gourmet Courgette 'Steak' Sandwich

From late June through to late September we have an abundance of courgettes. They are probably one of our most reliably prolific crops to the point that after adding them to every summer dish possible and blitzing them into bottles of passata, we still have had a big box of them available to place on the curbside, asking the locals to 'segíts magadon' - help yourself. Please!

I'm not sure what spurred Joe into creating this culinary masterpiece, but his tendency to be a little experimental certainly paid off in this case and has gone a long way to make a dent in our pile of courgettes. It may not sound like the most appetising of sandwich fillings - but give it a chance, once you have the juicy courgette goodness dripping down your chin I'm sure you'll be converted!

ingredients:
medium courgette
bread
oil
salt & pepper
ketchup
mustard
pickles/chutney of your choice
salad of your choice

Half the courgette and slice it lengthways to a

thickness of about 1cm. Heat a drizzle of oil in a frying pan and fry about two slices of courgette per sandwich. While the courgette is frying, season liberally with salt and pepper. The courgette is ready when it has softened and browned on both sides, but is still holding its shape.

Slice your bread - we recommend home-made wholemeal as it can take plenty of filling without getting soggy and falling apart in your hands. Load up your sandwich with enough slices of courgette to cover your bread, and then all the things you love - we recommend a squirt of ketchup and mustard; some chopped pickled chilli or a dash of hot sauce; slices of sweet pickled beetroot or other sweet chutney; and some salad - a slice of tomato, thinly sliced red onion and a rocket leaf or two work really well.

Grab a serviette and enjoy!

(We've recently discovered that once the courgettes are done and dusted, we can rely on thinly sliced and fried butternut squash or pumpkin for a just as delicious alternative steak sandwich!)

CHAPTER FIFTEEN

How does our garden grow?

"I wouldn't want to make it look like a gardener's garden, all clipped an' spick an' span, would you?" he said. "It's nicer like this with things runnin' wild, an' swingin' an' catchin' hold of each other."

"Don't let us make it tidy," said Mary anxiously. "It wouldn't seem like a secret garden if it was tidy."

The Secret Garden - Frances Hodgson Burnet

I serendipitously stumbled across this paragraph recently and it made me smile. I could see our current Hungarian garden in that century-old description. I could also see the faces of neighbours, friends and family - visitors to our little homestead over the years - who had been genuinely baffled that two people dedicating their life to the land, could be both proud and content with what, to them, looked an untended mess. It's not that we're after our very own secret garden (although I must admit that I find the unruly nature of our plots in mid-summer quite romantic), but rather that we know that Mother Earth works best when left to her own devices. Our approach to garden management differs significantly from the meticulous guidelines prettily photographed in RHS books or from the often contradictory advice given by a multitude of TV garden gurus, in that we are light touch - nurturing the soil and sowing the seeds, but not doing a whole lot more. Both Joe and I feel that we as humans have a fundamental responsibility to look after the planet that we live on. Part of this, for us, is to find the path least destructive - dropping the consumerist lifestyle, choosing to become vegan, growing our own food and doing our best to recycle, repair and reuse wherever possible. Unsurprisingly, our attitude toward managing our garden is very similar and leads us nicely to the practice of permaculture.

Permaculture is a fairly new term for the age-old practice of holistic, sustainable agricultural methods. These days, it stretches beyond agriculture and horticulture, but in the context of our little garden, this simplified definition is adequate. It's a balanced, symbiotic relationship between all things in the environment so as to keep the natural order going - kind of an 'I'll scratch yours if you scratch mine' arrangement. Outside of our garden, as agriculture has grown to meet the demands of rising populations, it's become increasingly industrial, destructive and ultimately unsustainable, so we're keen to counter that with a more gentle, natural approach Thinking that we are in control of everything in the great outdoors is a mistake and even attempting to control it can take a lot of hard work and prove to be frustrating and expensive. I've lost count of how many times people have commented on how hard we must work, that gardening involves such heavy labour, that they couldn't possibly bear the constant physicality of 'growing your own'. Yes, we can have some busy times, get our hands dirty and occasionally have tasks that can tone the muscles and get a sweat on, but arduous toil it certainly isn't. The bonus, although not the key reason for using permaculture techniques, is that working with nature actually takes much of the effort out of it.

We started off in Hungary quite inexperienced from a practical point of view. Joe brought plenty of knowledge from his horticulture degree, but a lot of what we've done here has been down to a little research and a lot of trial and error. We've accumulated a huge amount of real, hands-on experience from problems that we've faced and solutions that we've tried and tested. So we'd like to share them here, perhaps to save others the trouble, but at least to explain why we don't have 'a gardener's garden, all clipped an' spick an' span'!

We plan our plots and crops on an annual basis. Over winter we make decisions on what we want to plant and where everything should be positioned. The lay of the land is important - we consider what plots have more shade and which plants might prefer that; where there are tree roots that would prevent a decent root crop; where might be more sheltered from frost or more exposed to wind and which plots are higher or lower in the garden as we are on gently sloping land. The slope can be used to our advantage, for example, our most successful potato crop involved mounding them up with earth across the slope in order to create mini swales to capture the moisture that potatoes love, rather than it draining straight down the slope. We take care to choose seeds to suit our soil and climate rather than stubbornly choosing vegetables that we love but which simply will not grow no matter how much we manipulate their environment. I mean, I would love avocado and almond trees in the garden, but they simply wouldn't survive the harsh winters here, even if the summers are hot enough for them. We also consider companion planting and crop rotation, which I'll mention in more detail later.

There are a few key things that we do or *have* done, over late autumn and winter to prepare the soil for the seeds and seedlings come springtime. In our first couple of years, we had the strenuous but satisfying task of digging the entire garden over to clear it thoroughly from an accumulation of weeds and in particular the bindweed that seemed to be everywhere, strangling carrots, climbing up tomatoes and coiling deep through the earth like the 'devil's guts' that they're nicknamed. But across most of the garden the weeds seemed to calm a little after two years, leaving mainly grass, a few common weeds and a significantly reduced quantity of bindweed that we felt tolerable, so in our third year, we tried our hand at the no-dig technique. This, as its title cunningly suggests, involves leaving the ground undisturbed and therefore full of nutrients, bacteria and general goodness that needs to be maintained in healthy soil. Turning the ground increases the surface area exposed to air, sun and frost, all things which can be detrimental to the nutritional quality of the soil, which in turn is not so helpful for the plants that we're trying to grow there. The soil, after all, is the gardener's greatest asset and needs to be looked after. I don't think that we can honestly say that we've had higher or more quality yields as a result of this technique, although it has saved us digging the entire garden each autumn. More importantly, we feel that it is a way of caring for the soil that we're using year in, year out, rather than draining it of its goodness.

So while we're on soil, we should mention that the only thing we add to our garden every year is our very own compost, home-made behind a couple of upright wooden pallets in the corner of our garden. Spreading compost across the plots is the other important task that we ensure is done every winter before it freezes into an immovable solid heap. We love our compost! Throughout the year we accumulate all sorts of leftover kitchen waste, grass trimmings, leaves, failed preserves, rotten fruit, weeds. There are no rules for us - everything goes on there and everything rots down beautifully with no unpleasant smells. We don't turn it, cover it, layer it or worry about it, we just load it up and wait for it to magically transform. Come early winter we know that we can scrape off the top layers of more recent undecomposed stuff to reveal this gardener's gold and the satisfaction that we get from digging it out is immense. The wheelbarrow fills quickly with shovelfuls of rich, dark brown humus that looks like crumbled oxo cubes and smells earthy and mushroomy, like an autumnal walk in the woods. It's completely free, reduces the contents of our waste bins and goes a long way to rejuvenate the soil and put back what has been used over the spring and summer months - what's not to love?!

Once we have our multitude of seeds, most of which are bought over the winter months, we generally follow the seed packet instructions with regards to when and how to plant them. Occasionally we'll check up some information in one of our books or online and we'll always combine instructions with some common sense, for example, if we know of a predicted cold snap we'll hold off planting until the greatest risk has passed. We learned from our first year, and spying on our neighbour's techniques, to sow our seeds in greater quantities and closer together than suggested. If the plants end up crowded they can always be thinned down later and the spacing guidelines always seem to be geared up for those focused on winning a village prize, rather than more realistic, just as tasty, smaller vegetables. We always buy the cheapest seeds - they seem to work as well as those double, or quadruple the price.

Our garden is organic to the best of our ability. We use no pesticides or chemical fertilisers anywhere in the garden - our neighbours may use various sprayed or sprinkled potions and we can't help any inadvertent leaching of this stuff, but based on our garden's lively ecosystem, we think that we're doing pretty well. We can boast lizards, a cacophony of birds, butterflies, bees and wasps, preying mantis, insects of all shapes, colours and sizes, and more worms per square foot than we've seen in any soil. In fact, it's not unusual for our neighbour to ask what some bug or other is because they've never seen it in their own garden, just a few meters away. So what does being organic mean in terms of productivity? Well, we don't grow the biggest vegetables or have the greatest yields and of course, the risk of pests can mean that some produce is nibbled and it's not uncommon to find the odd cater-pillar in your greens. But the taste is always in-credible and I'd like to think that nutritionally it's some of the best food you could want to fuel your body. We've thought for a long time now that supermarket fruit and vegetables seem to be grown for their looks over their taste, watery and bland as they are, or never ripening. We, for-tunately, don't have that problem, and also have no worrying side effects from using chemicals.

There is an obvious disadvantage to not using pesticides, being that the pests absolutely love taking refuge in our chemical-free crops! We can, and do, take natural steps to help ourselves though. The first is crop rotation, which is a pre-ventative measure involving planting crops in different areas of the garden each year. Not only does this reduce the risk and recurrence of pest and diseases in a particular crop, but it's better for the soil not to have the same nutrients taken from it year after year by the same plant. Com-panion planting is also something that we con-sider. As the title suggests, this is planting crops together that are mutually beneficial to each other. Alliums such as onions next to carrots help to prevent carrot fly and planted between brassicas can reduce whitefly. Marigolds, nastur-tiums and other flowers are great to interplant between vegetables either as a deterrent or sim-ply to lure the pests away from the prized crop. Companion planting works in reverse too, where some crops should not be planted close together due to increased risk of similar pest or disease. We always plan our garden with these things in mind and it has generally worked well for us.

Of course, these are not fail-safe solutions and we have suffered some quite devastating infestations and problems over the past few years, some that we have been able to manage, and others where we have just had to throw our hands up and decide that we would go without a particular crop. In our first year, when I was particularly precious and melodramatic about my new seedlings, we had a terrible mole problem. Rows of young carrots and dwarf beans would be pushed up out of the ground, covered in soil and generally disturbed wreaking havoc on our potential crop. We did plenty of research, and not wanting to spend a fortune on expensive zapping machines, we sunk glass jars into the mole runs to create traps, which the moles theoretically would run into and be unable to turn around to escape. Moles apparently aren't that stupid. They diverted around the jars, apparently coming up to the surface more frequently, creating even more molehills to spite us. We poured water on the molehills. We even, bizarrely, buried musical candles in the mounds, having been advised (surprisingly not by a mole extermination expert, but by Joe's mum) that the high pitch tune is unbearable to their little furry ears. Don't bother with that one, it doesn't work! What did work, was human wee. This may sound unpleasant, but actually, Joe peeing onto the mounds made a definite impact. We noticed that the moles would find a different way around the garden, avoiding the pee-mounds and therefore also the baby beans. Persisting with this actually reduced our damages massively. The other way to get rid of moles is to acquire a cat - or several in our case. The only disadvantage to this is that moles apparently aren't a delicacy and don't get eaten by the cats, but rather are left littering the garden. Over the years of mole activity, I have actually come to appreciate the mole's role in the garden and the predator-prey relationship, noticing that the decrease in moles has directly correlated with the increase of slugs. It just goes to show that nature does know what it's doing and every creature has it's part to play. Except perhaps mosquitos, which I hate with a passion.

Aphids are a common problem for the average gardener and I knew from my childhood veg-patch that they can be sprayed off of plants with water, although this is something that needs to be done daily for some time. I was actually in the process of spraying our tomato plants in our first summer when I noticed something quite amazing. We have a lot of different ants in our garden, ranging from tiny specks to a giant variety that look more like spiders. We've had no problem with these multiple ants nests scattered around the crops, other than the odd bare foot being smothered with the bitey little critters when carelessly misplaced, but on the contrary, they have helped us hugely. What I saw on the tomato plants were lines of ants marching up the plant stems, grabbing one aphid at a time and carrying them back to the nest. They were taking care of pest control for us, the natural way. Again the predator-prey relationship helping us out without us even asking! Needless to say that the spray was put away and our trusty ants allowed for a bumper crop of juicy, sweet tomatoes.

We found out about Colorado beetles the hard way. We saw them on our potatoes before we knew what they were and if I remember rightly, spent some time admiring them and nicknaming them 'humbugs' due to their brown and cream striped shell. A day later our potatoes had no leaves. It was Sandor who helpfully pointed out that these bugs, and particularly their voracious plump, orange larvae, can decimate a potato crop in a matter of days. The following year we were on high alert for the humbugs and once just one was spotted we did a daily check for bugs and larvae, removing them and (unfortunately) squishing them as we quickly learned that the chickens wouldn't eat them. By our third year of potatoes, we were so efficient as spotting and removing the bugs and their little orange eggs, that the larvae never had a chance to do any damage of note. Combined with some strategically planted catnip, a natural bug deterrent, in ten minutes a day our potato pests were under control.

A persistent pest that was harder to control, particularly in our third year, were the slugs. Fond of hiding among the leaves of our jungly bean patch, they could be found by what seemed to be the hundred on cool, dewy mornings throughout summer. The battle for the beans, as it became known, involved precariously stepping through the thick undergrowth with a bucket as if we were playing a bizarre game of outdoor Twister, at the crack of dawn, picking slugs from leaves, stems and bean pods with our bare hands, trying not to crush any of our precious bean plants. It was not a particularly pleasant task, taking about half an hour each morning and leaving us with a bucket of brown slime-blobs and hands covered with a goo that took the rest of the morning to properly remove. The slugs were initially thrown to the chickens, but it quickly became clear that they were too big and too numerous for them to eat, so they were from then on thrown on the compost heap. There's no doubt that many of them made their way back to various other crops over the course of the night, but we just didn't know what else to do with them and certainly couldn't bring ourselves to dispose of them in some sort of horrific salt bath, even if it meant saving our precious vegetables. Salvation from the slugs may well be coming in the shape of a gaggle of hungry runner ducks. We've done some research and seen clips of these birds in action, employed in vineyards and fields around the world to keep crops pest free. Not only that, but some friends have been using them successfully at the garden of their ecolodge, and may have some chicks for us in the not too distant future.

Flea beetles are a new menace for us and have reinforced the fact that no year of crop growing is the same, whether it be the challenge of a different pest or disease, a late heavy frost or other extreme weather conditions. In this case, our brassica and tomato seedlings were decimated by these tiny, jumping dots of death, while still in the supposed safety of our polytunnel. The pure joy of noticing those first green shoots was completely quashed the following day after they had been chewed back to their stalks. We've not found a solution to flea beetles other than replanting again if there is time left in the season. We tried using a chilli or mint infusion over the crops as a deterrent to no avail and shaking the plants will disturb the infestation to a degree, but I'm not sure it does much to help in the long term.

Despite all of these challenges, we are continuously amazed at the resilience of plants. You just have to look at how quickly nature overruns derelict buildings to realise that plants will be here long after we've trashed everything else. This is why, for the most part, we are happy to leave nature to nurture our garden. In terms of ongoing care for our growing plants, its very low key. We water sporadically when needed, rather than religiously every day, so as to encourage roots to grow strong and deep, although we do increase the watering during very hot dry periods. Occasionally during these hot spells, we might use some light netting sheets as shade over young or delicate crops, but it's really quite impressive how the most wilted looking leaves can spring back to health once dusk creeps in.

The reason for my smile when reading the passage at the very beginning of this chapter comes down to our approach to weeding. Looking at our garden in midsummer you'll see a lot of green, in varied textures, heights and shades. You'll be able to make out rows of leeks and cabbages, there will be the wooden stakes poking up above the bushy tomato plants, the bean patch is a riot of tangled leaves and vines and the small trees break up the garden with their colourful fruit-laden branches. What you won't see is any earth. The neatly raked bare soil so common in our neighbours' gardens cannot be found anywhere. Those tidy English cottage gardens with orderly rows of weed free produce are not what we aspire to. We're not just being rebellious though, there is method to this madness. The grass, chickweed and other low-lying, shallow-rooted weeds provide the perfect living mulch to shade the soil from parching, retain moisture and prevent soil erosion during our heavy summer storms. This keeps the soil healthy and full of nutrients for our plants. I have to admit, I had some serious trouble signing up to this way of thinking in our first year and could regularly be found faithfully weeding down to the bare earth in order to keep the garden 'tidy' and free up our plants from the invading weeds. I found it difficult getting those images of weed-free rows of perfect vegetables in the gardening books out of my head - surely if the books say its the right thing to do, then its the right thing to do? Well, perhaps not. As heatwaves hit, the earth cracked, and sudden deluges of rain followed, so heavy that one year our onions were literally washed out of the earth. Then it all started to make sense. So we do weed our garden. But we weed down to a level below the planted crops so that there's no competition for light and space, but there remains a nice mat of greenery to hold everything together. It works well, saves the backbreaking work of removing every last shoot out of the ground and to me, looks tidy enough.

So the ground has been prepared, the seeds sown and the plants grown. The only thing left is to reap the rewards! We have found processing and preserving our fruit and vegetables to be, generally speaking, more time consuming and important than anything else. Every day from late spring we'll wander around the crops, inspecting what might be ready to pick. For the most part, our fruit and veg transitions from garden to plate very quickly, within minutes at some times of the year. We find that crops keep better on the plant and in the ground than in the pantry (or fridge, if you have one!) and so we pick leaves and fruit and dig roots up as and when we need them. There will be times when whole crops are ready at once or when we accumulate too many ripened fruit and veg, so we spend many an hour sterilising bottles and jars, making jams and passata, drying, fermenting and pickling. This happy process continues through to early autumn when the garden begins to empty as crops finish and empty plants are pulled up and thrown onto the compost heap. Occasionally we'll take the chance to collect seeds from the plants to reuse, although we've had mixed success. Tomato, chilli, squash, lettuce and various flower seeds seem quite productive, but chard and rocket seeds have produced plants that go straight to seed with minimal edible leaves. Still, this is not a great problem knowing how cheap new seeds are.

So, that's how our garden grows. I've grown to love this approach. Simple, cheap, sustainable ... and beautiful.

Classic Apple Crumble

We're lucky enough to have a good supply of different fruit available in our two gardens from strawberries, raspberries and cherries in June; gooseberries, apricots, peaches, pears and plums through mid and late summer, to apples in the autumn. Most of this fruit is good to use in one of the quickest, easiest and yummiest puddings there is, but here we'll stick with good old apple.

ingredients:
75g fat (butter or cooking margerine)
150g flour (I use half plain white and half whole-meal)
handful of oats
sprinkle of sugar
6-8 apples
spice (optional)

To make this medium sized crumble, suitable for four adult desserts, first start with your fruit. Any variety of apple can be used - ours are a selection as yet identified! Peel, core and chop your apples and soften gently in a pan with just a splash of water to prevent burning and a sprinkle of sugar. Add just a little spice of your choice to the softened fruit if you wish - cinnamon and cloves taste particularly good with apple. The fruit doesn't need to be cooked through as it will be going into the oven. Set aside while you make your crumble topping.

Put your fat and flour in a bowl, pinching and rubbing it together with your fingertips until you have fine 'breadcrumbs'. You'll find it much easier if the fat is cold. Once your mixture is nice and fine, throw in a handful or two of oats for flavour and texture and another sprinkle of sugar.

Spread the fruit in the bottom of a pie dish and cover evenly with crumble topping, sprinkling some more sugar over the top. Bake at a medium high heat for 30-40 minutes, until the topping is browned. Can be served warm with ice cream, cream or custard, but as Joe can testify, its just as moreish cold, eaten straight from the pie dish!

This dessert is so versatile. It can be made with a whole range of fruit, spices to suit your own preferences and can be scaled up or down easily, just remember to keep a ratio of double flour to fat for your topping.

CHAPTER SIXTEEN

Barefoot, beads and beans

I should make clear that I don't pretend to have even a modicum of medical education, but I feel that it would be remiss of me not to share some of the newfound knowledge that has had such a positive effect on our overall wellbeing since we changed our lifestyle. I wouldn't expect everyone, or anyone for that matter, to follow our lead in such a dramatic and total change, but if there are a couple of take-away snippets of thought provocation to spur on a change for the better for someone else, then it will have been worth the sharing.

Our Hungarian experience has allowed me to be in the privileged position of being able to compare 'befores' and 'afters' in my own mind and body. I can also look at friends and family, making observations based on their stories. Additionally, I'm an avid consumer of all sorts of information about the general contentment and welfare of society, and I am finding that the same

conclusions are being drawn time and again regarding the 'secrets' of building a long, healthy
and happy life. I am quite aware of the potential
for this to come across as happy-clappy hippie
nonsense ... but for me, for us, and for those
who have taken some inspiration in what we're
doing, this is pure and obvious common sense.
Sure, anyone can have a long life supported by
tablets and ongoing medical care ... but isn't happiness and health more important than longevity?

Okay, so I'll kick off with the tangible stuff;
the actual visible changes. My skin has become
clearer and healthier looking - I no longer have
the greasy sheen on my face that a day of work
in London used to generously provide me with.
Perhaps it's because I wear make-up so rarely
now, but I'd like to think it's because I'm living in
fresher, cleaner air rather than cutting through
exhaust fumes and general big city grime with
my face five days a week. I've even gone one
step further and stopped using face-cream on a
daily basis. It started as a trial for a week, to see
if I noticed any difference and on experiencing
none, decided that, in accordance with our frugal lifestyle, I would give up my Lidl brand day
and night creams altogether. Through winter I
might use the occasional blob of generic skin
cream, but otherwise, its been quite liberating
- considering that I've been on the face-cream
bandwagon from the tender age of thirteen. It's

not just my facial skin either, all over there has been a difference probably for the same reasons - not being coated in city grime, but instead being surrounded by clean air and sunshine, in which of course I spend the majority of my time, because of what we do. There is one other particular area that has noticeably improved, that being my 'nether regions'. Yes, it's all very Channel 4 'embarrassing bodies', but I found it quite interesting that within a few weeks of escaping my office job, the skin on my butt was, well, smooth as a baby's bottom. Perhaps it was my body's way of telling me to get off my arse and change things up? I'm not in the practice of talking to all of my friends about the state of their bums, but I wouldn't at all be surprised if this is a problem encountered by many a student, office worker or anyone in a sedentary profession.

Aside from better skin, we both also found that we were getting toned, trim and feeling good through simple daily tasks like working in the garden and going for decent length dog-walks. We added to these gentle, accidental workouts with more planned exercise - daily yoga and the occasional cycle, sometimes for fun, sometimes to cut petrol costs. We embrace the outdoors whenever we can, getting back to our roots, in summer walking barefoot on the earth and grass, regularly exposing our bodies to healthy, natural bacteria. Particularly in our 'first world' urban lives, we are over-protected from everything, living in rather a sterile world, shielded from any soil on our veggies or dirt in our homes. Joe and I have fortunately never become ill since we moved to Hungary. We have both ditched our asthma inhalers and take no medication other than the occasional paracetamol or ibuprofen for a headache or muscle strain. The only time we have visited our local doctor, three years into our time here, was because we got stopped by the police and had to get a medical examination and papers in order to get a Hungarian drivers license. We've not had flu and don't get the long drawn out winter colds that we used to get in the UK, where the cough lingers for weeks even after the sore throat and sniffles disappear. And this is in colder climes and in a house with no central heating. I think its fairly safe to say that we've never felt healthier than we do right now.

Time is most certainly a factor in our healthier lives, a luxury that we have in abundance. In our new lives, we have chosen to prioritise time over wealth and status, and its a decision that has served us well. We have time in our day, every day, for exercise, reading, self-education, and hobbies that were always sacrificed before due to a lack of time. We have time to listen to what our bodies and minds are telling us. If we feel an ache or a slight sniffle, we rest up and look after ourselves instead of battling on with work. Time also allows us to sow, grow, pick and cook our own food.

Our diet has been through a few changes since living in Hungary too. For the most part, this has been a reaction to our environment rather than a proactive decision to eat more healthily, but either way, we feel that it's played a big part in our improved health and happiness. Growing your own food means seasonal eating and ensures that food is as fresh as it can be, sometimes going from garden to plate within minutes. And having the time to prepare it properly from scratch sees it used as nourishment for the body rather than a quick fix to fill the hole in your tummy. Reconnecting with our food has been hugely positive, but has also brought about some changes that I never thought would happen. We had already decreased our meat intake due to our lack of fridge and freezer, but a massive change was the decision to become vegetarian after we could no longer accept that killing our rabbits for food was an okay thing to do. Then a bombshell of dairy-based education hit us with our goat experience and shortly afterwards we became vegan. It feels amazing not putting animal products in your body. Not just physically with the reduction of bloating, inflammation and lethargy after meals, but psychologically too. We couldn't continue to support the dairy and egg industries knowing what we learned and researched. There are a hundred and one superb films explaining the benefits of veganism, so I needn't preach here to either the converted or the unwilling. But for us, we feel great with a slight loss of weight and more energy all around. It's cheaper, simpler and has seen us eating a way more varied, interesting and nutritional diet than ever before. We don't focus on micro-nutrients because we know that as long as we keep it varied we'll get everything that we need - and actually, the average omnivore is just as likely to be missing key nutrients as any vegan, particularly fibre. Oh, and water, lots and lots of water to stay hydrated - so simple but essential for body and mind and so often taken for granted.

So I've covered the physical stuff, but there's something arguably more important that we feel that we're just mastering, and that's the psychological stuff. Its so important to look after your mental health, more so in today's social media-fuelled, busy, noisy first-world lives. There are so many pressures placed on us in modern society - we have to get an education, hold down a good job, pay bills, have a stable relationship, be a good mum, dad, partner, friend, have copious amounts of filter-photographed fun and look good at all times. We are being subconsciously programmed by the glossy marketing everywhere we turn, from the TV in our own home to billboards and shopfronts, newspapers and radio. The thing is, that this marketing is not even trying to be positive half of the time

- on our rare trips back to the UK we realised we were hypersensitive to the scaremongering on the TV, with ads for funerals, insurance, drugs and health cures. It could make you worry so much about dying that you could forget to live. There's limited room to be calm and quiet and content with what we have, here in the present.

So we have removed ourselves. Not completely - I still listen to the radio and I'm a sucker for some scrolling through Facebook, but we have control over it. We have deliberately simplified our lives. We don't have a lot of 'stuff' and because of where and how we live, there is very little pressure to keep up with the Jones's. Initially, I was worried about being tied to one place for a long time and not having the budget for ongoing holidays, having been used to travelling as much as I wanted to. But what I've found is that we don't crave the holidays. We don't feel the need to have a 'break' from anything because what we're doing is so enjoyable. Our pace of life and ability to do more or less whatever we want to every day means that there's no striving to escape or rest. It took a little while to adjust, but we've learned to appreciate the value of wandering around our garden in the sunshine, breathing fresh air and taking time to ponder on what might need doing that day. We have time and space to be calm and mindful of our actions. Life is quieter, both literally and figuratively - the air is emptier of noise and bustle but in theory, anyone could move to a quieter place if they can afford a cottage in the country … sometimes it's life that needs to quieten, rather than the environment.

Stress is a killer and stressed bodies are susceptible to all sorts of problems. It can lead to so many illnesses both directly and indirectly. It can raise blood pressure, lower the immune system and affect the quality of sleep, something that is hugely underestimated for overall health. We've managed to create a fairly stress-free haven for ourselves here in Hungary, by removing those things that we identified as causing us the greatest problems. For me, it was working every day at a job that I had absolutely no passion for and for Joe it was living in a society that was over-crowded and materialistic. Different things will trigger stress in different people, but if you can identify the trigger and then go some way to remove or reduce it, then the stress can be managed.

Perhaps its the lack of stress that also allows us to sleep so well, although I must admit that I've always been lucky to be the kind of person that could fall asleep standing up on the train if I really wanted to. Sleep is so very important - and good quality sleep where the brain has a chance to work its overnight magic. A while ago, to give Joe and I a break from each other over the bleak Hungarian winter, I treated myself to a week-long yoga retreat in Andalucia, a chance to improve on my self-taught home yoga techniques and meet some like-minded people. I was absolutely amazed to find that not one of the girls on the retreat were good sleepers. They seemed to revel in their stories of how they never got a good night's sleep, they suffer from horrific nightmares, can't get comfortable, wake every hour. They also talked about their high stress levels, mostly due to work or finances. I found it disconcerting how blase they were about it, almost like it was a new fashion trend and I was, as always, odd-girl-out. I felt like screaming 'SURELY THIS IS NOT NORMAL?'. Whether its normal or not in their minds, sleep is essential for a properly functioning brain and body.

There's a bit of a Catch-22 when it comes to sleep. Stress can create poor sleep patterns and then those poor sleep patterns, in turn, create increased stress - a bit of a vicious circle. Our lifestyle has no doubt supported general healthy sleeping habits - a regular routine of getting up at dawn and chilling out from dusk, fresh air and exercise during the day, and maybe occasional gentle yoga or meditation in the evening if we fancy it. Research regularly shows the obvious stuff like eating before bedtime, alcohol, coffee, TV, devices and other stimulants are not great sleepytime companions, so we ditch these if sleep is not coming easy. A drop of lavender oil on the mattress and some soft mellow music is super soothing when needed.

Finally, something that I have stumbled across recently but I suppose have always subconsciously been aware of is the Japanese concept of 'ikigai'. This translates roughly as 'a reason for being' - a raison d'etre, a purpose. Its particular to each individual person and once this pursuit has been found, it allows the individual to find a mental state of ease and contentment and consequently a feeling of finding the meaning of life - I like to think of it as finding your flow. Before I read anything about ikigai, I would often find myself wandering the garden for hours at a time in spring and summer, completely absorbed in checking the vegetable plots, looking for pests, weeding around the tomatoes and fussing over the animals. It would bring me such joy, peace and contentment that I would feel happy right to the bottom of my heart. I get the same feeling when I'm washing the dishes, hanging the laundry and other fairly menial tasks that fit together as part of keeping the little homestead running, but also when I'm engaged in more creative activities, like building our mud pizza oven or super-sized bug hotel and even writing this book! The point is, that having something that gives you a reason for being is good for the soul and in Japan has been linked to improved happiness and longevity. You may well have a hobby or interest in which you find your flow already and if so it should definitely be nurtured; but if there is currently nothing in your life bringing a deep seated satisfaction, it may well pay to find something - whether it be running, knitting, gardening, or some social activity or other, there is clearly something beneficial about discovering your own raison d'etre!

To summarise, we - the collective human 'we' - largely know what to do in order to lead a happy and healthy life; its just a matter of *how* to do it, ditching the excuses and having that willingness to change if things aren't working. After all, things aren't going to change themselves - there's that saying about how the definition of crazy is doing the same thing over and over again and expecting different results. Well ... there you have it.

Beanfeast Burgers With Pan Fries

Veggie burgers have become a staple of our cooking repertoire in a way that meat burgers never did. Its probably because the variations are almost endless - I'd be hard pressed to say that I've made exactly the same burger twice because the contents of our garden and pantry are ever changing. This also makes them a great choice for using up those seemingly random items left in the cupboard and fridge. They're always delicious, simple to make and are a hearty, healthy option. And its not just the ingredients that are flexible - once made, the burger mix can be used to create sausages, meatballs or even the filling to a pastry covered vegetable wellington!

ingredients:
1 can (or cooked equivalent) pinto, borlotti or kidney beans, drained
1 medium grated carrot
1 medium grated beetroot
chopped garlic
tbs soy sauce
salt & pepper
½ tsp ground chilli
ground paprika
ground cumin
oats

potatoes
oil for frying

burger buns and garnish if you want the full burger experience!

Throw all of the burger ingredients, except the
oats, together and blitz to a paste using a stick
blender or food processor. Feel free to taste
the mix and adjust the spices and seasoning to
suit you, there's no raw meat here afterall! Add
enough oats (fine ground work best) to bind
everything and dry the mixture to a suitable
burger pattie consistency. If your mix seems wet
after adding quite a lot of oats, try adding a
few tablespoons of flour. Shape the burgers into
the size rounds that you require (remembering
that the thicker they are, the longer the cooking
time), place on a baking paper lined tray, and
leave to stand while you prepare your potatoes
and wait for your oven to heat up.

Wash the potatoes and cube them to roughly
1cm - leaving the skin on means extra flavour.
Heat some oil in a heavy frying pan and add
the potatoes when hot, taking care of spitting
or splashing oil. They will need unsticking from
the pan and turning every few minutes but not
continuous stirring.

Drizzle the burgers with oil and put them in the
oven - they'll need around 40 minutes to become brown and slightly crispy on the outside.
Turn them once halfway through cooking.

The potatoes should be ready at about the same
time as the burgers, when they are golden and

crispy. Serve the burgers on a bun with all the usual trimmings - salad, fried onions and sauces, with the pan fries on the side, sprinkled with a little salt.

*note - I mentioned at the start that there are a lot of variations to this burger mix. My general observation is that if you include the 'magic 3' combination of 1) cooked beans/cooked pulses/ tofu, together with 2) fresh grated vegetables or mushrooms and then a binding ingredient of 3) oats, breadcrumbs or flour, then you should have the basis of a great burger that you can season any way you want. Have an experiment!

EPILOGUE

So we've been through five summers, five autumns, four winters and four springs at our Hungarian homestead. Although each year has been quite different, we've settled into the seasonal changes quite happily, perfecting the growing and harvesting of our crops and becoming ever more content with the simplicity of things here, even if we're not quite as self-sufficient as we'd like to have been.

We acquired a pair of Indian runner ducks as chicks from some friends who run an ecolodge in the south of the country and from small, fluffy, kiwi-like beginnings they grew into quite elegant, beautiful birds who have proved their worth many times over through efficient pest control in the garden. Unfortunately they are also incredibly messy, needing their sleeping area cleaned out far more often then the chickens ever did; and also just a little dim-witted, scared of their own shadow and unable to understand how fences work - occasionally trying to push or fly through them and when unable to, the pair of them sit next to each other with the wire between them as if on a prison visit. Despite their stupidity though, the male still manages to rule over Penfold in a way none of our other animals ever have - its not uncommon to have to come out to save the dog, who has been backed into a corner of the garden, unable to escape from those dangerous ever-quacking beaks. We no longer have any chickens, as one of our final pair suddenly died and we couldn't bear the other to be lonely so we gave her away to a friend with a small group of hens. Our ever-fluctuating number of cats now sits at three - Fergusson (the mama) and two of her daughters - and they all love Penfold, even if he is more fickle, only really considering Fergus to be a true friend. We have no plans for any other animals at this stage, but I do miss having them.

After four years of struggling with the language, we've finally found ourselves a fabulous Hungarian teacher. He lives in the village and despite being the local English teacher and tutor, he knew nothing about the two crazy English people that lived 10 minutes walk away from him until we were introduced (frustratingly by someone we met in our first year here - why did he wait so long?!). We spend two hours every Tuesday chatting away in English and learning plenty of Hungarian grammar, vocabulary and also picking up tips on common language, culture, history and even some recipes thanks to his lovely wife. Its been a fabulous bonus, albeit late, and we hope he sees fit to keep teaching us for free for as long as it takes for us to construct some decent sentences!

And finally, near enough to the month that our

original five year plan comes to an end, we have some solid plans of packing our panniers, leaving Penfold with his 'grandparents' and cycling off into the horizon for several weeks of vegan fuelled, low budget cycling across the Balkans. Bring on the adventures!

Acknowledgements

I would like to thank all my friends and family for providing me with the love and encouragement to continue writing the blog that has eventually turned into this book. You know who you are!

We have an assortment of various gardening and horticulture books accumulated over the course of Joe's degree - all of them are helpful in one way or another, but the following few books are those that I have referred to in my writing, and those that are particularly pertinent to our way of life.

The one straw revolution - Masanobu Fukuoka
The secret garden - Frances Hodgson Burnett
John Seymour - The Complete Book of Self-Sufficiency
Ikigai: The Japanese secret to a long and happy life - Hector Garcia & Francesc Miralles

Printed in Great Britain
by Amazon